SEVEN ATTRIBUTES OF
HIGHLY EFFECTIVE
DEVELOPMENT VENDORS

Secrets to establishing a successful client/vendor relationship

WILLIAM V. WEST

First printing 2014
Printed in the United States

ISBN 978-0-9916441-1-7

Reviews From The Industry

"Working for a large global corporation, it is always difficult to find vendors who truly understand the cultural intricacies of working across multiple geographical markets. I worked with Bill on a project outsourcing learning design and development services for a 250,000+ people organization, throughout North America, Europe and APAC. From start to finish Bill demonstrated a first class understanding of people, cultures and processes, making the transition as painless as possible."
> **– Mark Noviss**
> **Vice President at J.P. Morgan**

"I have had the pleasure of working with Bill on some of the initiatives discussed in the book. Bill is a top notch learning professional and he hits the mark with the seven attributes. The learning space is highly fragmented and with no barriers to entry learning companies that are ill prepared to meet the demands of their clients are disruptive to our industry."
> **– Don Duquette**
> **Executive Vice President, Learning Solutions**
> **at GP Strategies Corporation**

"We were struggling with our development strategies, and Bill helped us find the right path by confronting the mismatch in expectations and capabilities. His expertise, laid out so well in this book, is invaluable."
> **– George Brennan**
> **Chief Learning Officer at Intel**

"Bill understands that the successful partnership in learning outsourcing extends well beyond org charts and processes. He addresses the need to weave methodology, experience, infrastructure, and innovation into the decision making process, then how to leverage these attributes as the relationship comes to life. His case draws out the important nuances that can tilt a relationship towards success and away from failure."

– Michael Papay
CEO at Fort Hill Company

"If you're looking for a route map to successful vendor selection, this is it. Based on 25 years of practical experience, full of anecdotes and insightful observations, West charts a pragmatic path to partnership. 'Alignment' is a word that stands out in this book: alignment between partners, but this alignment doesn't come about by chance. This book provides a route map to partnership, seven core factors that you need to consider, and a highly pragmatic and practical approach."

– Julian Stodd
Founder and Co-Captain at SeaSalt Learning

"Bill is one of the most knowledgeable professionals in learning product development that I've had the pleasure to work with. I witnessed how his company Option Six delivered outstanding learning product development projects. Every project was on time, on budget and realized its vision. Those results could only be realized by a dedicated team, with an effective methodology and effective tools. Bill truly knows what it takes to build and run a highly effective learning development organization."

– Eckhart Boehme
former Curriculum Architect Marketing@Microsoft,
Corporate Marketing Group at Microsoft Corp.

"Early in my career at a major technology company, I had to locate a company that I could trust and partner with to meet my business needs. I have worked with lots of vendors over the years so I knew what I needed. After being referred to Option Six and talking to Bill, I felt confident his team could bail me out of my training fire drill. I was right. I needed a training solution that met my manager's high expectations and helped us create business impact with a timely launch to 70,000 employees. My job was on the line and so was my business. Option Six jumped right into the fire with me and through their expertise, innovative design and true partnership, we saved the day together. "Thanks for saving my team's job, Bill!"

> **– Evelyn Jackson**
> **Worldwide Operator Channel Readiness Manager**
> **at Microsoft**

"My advice to readers, absorb this book, don't just read it! Bill expertly lays out the reality and necessary rigor required to successfully manage the learning and development vendor partnership. Bill has proven to me the value of his experience, standards of practice, and trusted partnership in three companies…. a track record of high profile successes, issues well resolved, and no failures."

> **– Rob Bateman**
> **President & Senior Partner at Strategic Talent Solutions**
> **and Former Vice President of Training and Organization**
> **Development at Krispy Kreme**

"There is perhaps no one more expert to write on the subject of managing learning development vendors than Bill West. In these pages, Bill shares decades of wisdom and experience in the learning space, and candidly reveals his trials, successes, and learnings when dealing with vendors, all with the intention of helping CLOs and learning leaders avoid the pitfalls when selecting, working with, and managing learning development vendors. A highly revealing and readable book for all learning leaders who need a mentor and ally in this area."

> **– Larry Strasner**
> **Manager of Trainer Services at The Training Associates**

"Bill West has taken on a key challenge in learning and development—finding the right vendor to develop a mission-critical training initiative. And he is the right man for the job, able to draw on his extensive experience to elucidate the seven attributes that make or break the success of outsourced development programs and to illustrate them with a wide range of examples and case studies."

> **– Roy V.H. Pollock, DVM, PhD**
> **Chief Learning Officer at The 6Ds Company**

"While at Option Six, Bill's team built the Brandon Hall award-winning program Foundations of High-Tech Marketing for Chasm Institute. Our clients were the ultimate beneficiary of best practices in development management that are described in The Seven Attributes for Highly Effective Development Vendors."

> **– Mark Cavender**
> **Founder and Managing Director at Chasm Institute LLC**

"I do a lot of work with contract suppliers in my role. From my very first meeting with Bill, I knew our high visibility project would go well. Every subsequent encounter with his company confirmed my initial judgment. He had figured out how to strike the right balance between engaged leadership and staff empowerment. The fact that we won an industry award for the final product was almost a foregone conclusion."

> **– Glenn Fourie**
> **Director in the Strategic Enterprise Architecture Group at Microsoft**

"Bill West is one of the best business partner's I have collaborated with over my 14 years as an entrepreneur in the learning and development industry. He possesses a unique combination of vision, pragmatism and discipline that creates an environment in which mutual success is the result and delighting clients is the reason. I can think of no better person to share advice regarding the systematic approach and identification of vendors who grow to become partners."

> **– Christopher J. Quinn**
> **Founder of Imprint Learning Solutions**

"Bill West has years of experience in delivering effective learning. He's distilled that experience into a thoughtful analysis of the training development process and seven principles that will ensure a win/win relationship between a buyer and a training vendor. Winning means a training project that meets a company's business requirements while ensuring the vendor makes a profit and can be around for the next project. The seven principles are a clear guide to ensuring a win/win training delivery."

> **– Terry Heiney**
> **President and Founder at The Learning Network**

"As a vendor, Bill's company reflected something found rarely in others I had used in the past. For me, I found operational excellence as a standard of practice. This book reflects Bill's dedication to operational excellence and serves to inform a viable future to any training industry professional striving to operationalize success in building sustained workforce capability."

> **– Gary Wise**
> **Learning and Performance Solutions Strategist at Xerox**
> **and Former Director Sales Training, Learning Methods**
> **& Technologies at Roche Diagnostics**

Who is this book for?

This book is for everyone who has ever had to select an outsource vendor, especially those who will have to select one in the future. It provides a prescriptive framework for selecting a vendor that fully meets your needs and enables you to establish a highly successful client/vendor relationship. Seven Attributes is groundbreaking and takes an innovative approach to making both you and your vendor successful.

About This Book

I've been fortunate. Over the past 25 years, I've had the fortune
of including some of the most respected companies as my
employers—IBM, Accenture, Ernst & Young (EY), GP
Strategies, and Xerox—and many of the world's most admired
companies as my clients. These clients include over 50
companies in the Fortune 500, 18 in the Fortune 150, and the
largest company in 11 of the major industry sectors. A few of my
more noteworthy clients have included (alphabetically): 3M,
Amway, AT&T, Bank of America, Cisco, HP, Intel, Johnson
& Johnson, Kraft, Krispy Kreme, Lilly, Lowe's, Microsoft,
NBC/Universal, Papa John's, Pfizer, Prudential, Roche,
SunTrust, and Toyota, among others.

I use the term fortune instead of luck. Luck tends to imply
something joyful. My fortune was often joyful, but not always.
I was lucky in 2000, when the much-heralded UNext.com, which
had been financed to the tune of $200 million, decided to open

a development center for their online MBA curriculum in my hometown of Bloomington, Indiana, and that the vice president in charge was a former partner of mine at Andersen Consulting. That was joyful. However, the joy wore off in 2001, when UNext burned through their funds, the market bubble burst, two buildings in New York collapsed, UNext shut down our operation, and I was left with 40 employees wondering what was next for them. I would eventually build from those remnants the very successful e-learning company, Option Six. That was a fortune that propelled me to where I am today. Over the next 10 years, I would amass the majority of my clients and the cases in this book.

In the spring of 2013, I was asked to present at the CLO Symposium. As mentioned, I've been around the training industry for a very long time. I present for many clients and forums on the latest innovations within training, such as mobile learning, social learning, virtual instructor-led training, and so on. In this particular case, because the audience consisted of chief learning officers, I wanted to pick a topic that was uniquely "me." I wanted to pick a topic where I could combine my unique experiences and offer something useful to the audience, but also a topic that I knew I could defend. It's impossible to predict what you might get into with the question-and-answer session at a conference of this nature, so I wanted to make sure I could pick a topic that was bulletproof. That's when I came up with the concept of the Seven Attributes.

I dug into my archives, evaluated lots of my case studies, considered many of the successes and failures that I had witnessed, thought about the things that I personally had achieved, and set forth to try to define one of the most important aspects of our business: training development outsourcing. The topic I proposed was "The ten attributes to demand from your training development vendor." As it turns out, ten was a very ambitious number. As I dug deep, I realized that I didn't need ten. Seven was ample. Seven managed to encapsulate everything that I felt was important in selection of a training development provider. This was a topic with which I felt very comfortable. I was constantly involved with proposal development over the past dozen years as an entrepreneur. They ranged from small ones as a result of one-on-one conversations with clients to the large ones as a result of an industry-scale RFP, everything from a $10,000 course to a $5 million annual, multi-year relationship.

During the 18 months prior to the presentation, I was on a winning streak. I had won five of the largest RFPs in the training industry at that time. However, the area where I thought I was strongest was not simply "winning" the account, but "operationalizing" it—meaning the ability to go into the client environment, understand the needs, assemble a team, and produce amazing results that would lead to what I call an "enthusiastic approval."

For the CLO conference, this would be a unique topic. This was an area where I thought I could offer something special, because this is one of the biggest areas of pain for training departments, finding the right provider and praying that it will work. In the presentation, I defined **"success"** as **the equilibrium when the client has his vision realized and the vendor makes a profit.** In that situation, magical things can happen.

So I gave my presentation, and it went so well that I started a new company. It's really that simple. This is a massive issue in our industry, and I believe I've designed a formula for solving it. The audience included companies that I would refer to as "buyers" and training development consultants that I would refer to as "providers." The reception was equally warm from both sides because both sides feel the pain when the relationship doesn't work.

Several members of the audience came to me afterward. The comments were varied: Some were terrified because they were about to launch an RFP, and in many ways, their jobs were on the line. One attendee from a very large corporation who approached me was frustrated because their vendor relationship was going horribly. His statement was "I wish I had heard your presentation before we made our decision." One gentleman who had just been appointed the CLO was in the process of defining his strategic plan approached me. He looked at the outline of my presentation and said, "That's my strategic plan."

I am quite confident that understanding the Seven Attributes will lead you to developing a highly effective training development organization and selecting your best outsourcing partner.

Let's stop here and discuss the vernacular I use in this book. The word *training* has been used for centuries to reflect how one individual builds the abilities of another. However, the word *training* is unpopular in our industry. As the saying goes, "*you train animals, not people.*" Instead, we use terms like performance, education, learning, content, instruction, development, and others to reflect the solutions that we build. That's all reasonable and accurate, but it produces a major challenge when writing a book and determining how to consistently refer to our domain and solutions without criticism. So, for the sake of this text, I will continue to use the term *training* to refer to the industry while applying the additional terms when more aligned with each usage. When in doubt, I'll still use training, and you'll simply have to indulge me.

So Why Is This Book Important?

There is a crisis in this industry. The problem that we currently face within the training industry is that there is an extremely high failure rate in training development (content development, learning development, solutions development, etc.). The success rates for internal development groups are always under scrutiny, but the success rates for outsourcing initiatives has reached a level that affects the ability for the industry to function effectively. Do I have statistics? No, I do have statistically reliable data that states the percentage of outsourcing deals that have been successful. My statements are purely based on my own observations over the past 13 years in the training industry. However, let me qualify this a bit and lay out some pretty strong empirical data. In 2001, I founded and grew one of the industry's most successful content development companies, Option Six, which won more than 20 international awards and built a *Who's Who* client list. I sold my company to one of the largest providers in the training industry, spent 2.5 years as a vice president with them, and after a brief sabbatical, assumed a position as senior vice president with one of the other largest providers.

Overall, I oversaw the outsourcing relationships of over 50 clients and completed hundreds of courses, perhaps over one thousand. I listed some of my clients earlier. No lightweights here.

So why do I have such a negative viewpoint toward the success rate? First, with nearly every new client, when we were hired to partner with a client, we were replacing the former vendor. Some of these were small $20,000-$50,000 accounts, while others were multimillion dollar campaigns. Too often, it was in the twilight of a disaster—not a good sign for them. Second, we had a chance to observe many other development vendors, hearing their stories either directly or via mutual clients. I noted what worked, and what did not, and I used the insight to improve my own company.

Let me also point out that the boutique firms in our industry are not nearly as competitive as the larger providers (who are seriously cutthroat). The boutiques are collegial. We're all trying to survive, and there is always enough business to go around, so we share our stories. As a relatively small development company in the early days, we watched as the giants in the industry would take over large-scale outsourcing operations, and then we observed their successes and failures. Finally, once I sold my own company and joined the ranks of the larger firms, I saw a broader array of cases within my new employer and within other competitors with mutual clients. I've been at the helm of some of the largest victories in the industry and witness to some of the historic failures.

One of my favorite failure stories is the outsourcing attempt by a major pharmaceutical company. They fired their prime vendor after 7 years and replaced them with another provider who, after 12 months, had to pay the client a $1M refund for services that failed to achieve their objective. In my view, all three parties failed. No one achieved the vision, and no one made any money. There's much room for improvement in our industry.

The issue starts and ends with **standards of practice.** Unlike accounting, legal software development, manufacturing, architecture, medicine, and so many other professions, the training industry has no standards. There is no clearly defined and accepted qualification to become an instructional designer. There is no process or methodology that is detailed to the point where we can all follow it without making mistakes—one that's based on tried-and-true best practices. **Finally, there is no existing platform that allows us to do our work and pull everything together in one place.** Human resource professionals have tools like Oracle, PeopleSoft, and SAP. Many other professions have similar ERP systems that allow them to do everything that needs to be done within their processes. The training industry does not have this. We must resort to homegrown solutions using spreadsheets, project management software, and other tools—none of which talk to each other.

So we have an industry with a widely diverse employee-base, where each person must define his own processes, based on this widely diverse background-set, and where people must create their own tools to support them. And we wonder why we have issues with quality? Extrapolate that to outsourcing. Every vendor has its own hiring standards, processes, and toolsets. Some are good. Some are bad. No two are the same. So we play *spin the bottle* with vendors until we find one who can get the job done.

Envisioning the Seven Attributes

What would a world feel like if everyone in your company produced training in the same manner and all your vendors were following the same process? How would your life improve if every course produced shared a common level of quality, was completed on time, and the team, SMEs, and learners all enjoyed the process? This is where improvement is most needed and where I believe my personal experience provides the most value. Many of the techniques in this book can be applied to the selection of a training development provider, but they are also applicable lessons for improving any training organization, whether it is an internal learning and development (L&D) or outsource provider.

I refer to this framework as the *Seven Attributes of Highly Effective Development Vendors.* They are, in order of importance, **Experience, Methodology, Infrastructure, Process, Technology, Talent,** and **Innovation.** These are the attributes by which we can categorize the characteristics, tools, and techniques that are needed to produce highly effective solutions and strong outsourcing relationships. The Seven Attributes nicely compartmentalize those things that really make a difference.

In my career, I have been fortunate to have been exposed to so many organizations that produced excellent results, while also witnessing countless other organizations that have struggled. We see pockets of successes and failures almost everywhere we go. The question I've sought to answer is this: What makes one initiative succeed while another one fails?

My career experience—those companies where I have been employed, companies I have founded, and companies that have hired my teams to support them—has given me exposure to a vast array of business models. It has populated my vault of case studies with examples of successes and failures within the many scenarios that we all face day to day. I will use these case studies as a means of outlining best practices throughout this book. I haven't seen it all, but I have seen so much!

This book is organized into three primary sections. The first section is an assessment of the current situation to help you really understand the basics of how outsourcing works, how vendors are selected, and the vendor's business. The second section dives into the Seven Attributes. For each attribute, I outline a variety of scenarios that have failed, a definition of what that attribute entails, examples of successes and best practices, and provide tools when I can. The third section addresses the selection of vendors and how the RFP process works from the vendor's perspective. I also include some critical questions that you should ask during the RFP process, I cover effective pricing strategies, and I attempt to get into the reality and beyond the standard *pomp and circumstance* of the proposal process.

Nobody works for free. I have a family to feed. I make my living as a consultant and running a company that helps organizations improve their overall maturity, apply the Seven Attributes, and implement an infrastructure that allows them to be effective. My contact information is in this book, so I certainly welcome any and all inquires either online, as a way of continuing our dialogue in our industry, or personally if I may be of some assistance to you. Enjoy!

Table of Contents

Preface

Preface

If you are a large corporation and it is time to select your auditor—the person who will ensure that your financials are within legal compliance requirements—you probably have some high expectations as to the one you select. You have an expectation about their educational level. You expect that they have passed their certification exams. You expect that they are following the same processes that any other auditor might follow and that they have some sort of systems infrastructure to keep everything organized. You are unlikely to hire an auditor whose primary qualifications were their knowledge of QuickBooks and their experience managing their family business. That just is not acceptable. Not for your business. It would be dangerous! Your financial statements and your accountability are exceptionally important, as are the taxes that you must pay. A simple mistake could be very costly. A big mistake could be disastrous.

Yet, what do we do in the training industry? We don't have expectations on the educational level of our instructional designers (IDs). We don't have certification exams that IDs are expected to pass before practicing. There is no standard process that you can expect everyone to follow while developing your training, and there is not a platform that anyone can use that will manage from end to end all the tasks that are conducted as part of training development.

What happens in an environment like this? Executives in the organization challenge the return on investment for training, business units struggle to get things accomplished because training is not available on time, the subject matter experts don't like the instructional designers, and vice versa. The learners don't see the value in the training they're told to take, and it's impossible to keep up with new innovation.

INEFFECTIVE TRAINING. INEFFECTIVE BUSINESS.

Training touches every aspect of a business. It is through training that the employees of the business know how to do their jobs, have the possibility of doing their jobs better and are able to stay out of trouble (i.e., compliance regulations). Without effective training, product doesn't roll out on time, systems implementations fail, compliance rules are violated, strategic initiatives fail to achieve their vision, and new employees do not know how to do their jobs. Almost every major initiative in your business is affected by training.

If training is effective then, frankly, most people don't notice it. They consume it and are able to move forward and do their business, without hesitation. I used to describe this scenario as such: "The client is trying to run their business—they have something they want to achieve. Once they are ready, they want to cross their arms, blink their eyes, and have the training magically appear. That's where we come in." That's where every training organization—internal learning and development organization and development outsourcing company—comes in. But the training has to be effective.

I've had a chance to see some fantastic successes and I've been witness to some dramatic failures. Those successes that I've seen are directly related to the company and/or the vendor being fully aligned across the Seven Attributes; though it is only recently that I have categorized this alignment into this model. These successes are a result of having high expectations to the educational and experience level of their staff, having a strong consistent process across all their organizations, a methodology that they all believe in and know how to practice, and backend systems that allows people to do their jobs without manual processes or spreadsheets.

On the other hand, the failures almost always involve the experience level of the employees, the inadequacy of the process, the working relationship between the client and vendor, including between companies and their own subject matter experts, and the lack of an integrated data flow throughout the project.

Throughout this book I will not endorse any specific providers, nor will I demonize. I would love to promote the companies and the vendors that were party to some of the great successes that I've seen, but I want to be consistent because I won't cite those that were responsible for the failures that I witnessed. I will give you short generic backgrounds on the parties involved, such as their industry, the size of the company, and other identifiable information for context to allow you to categorize the organization and identify for yourself the relevance towards your circumstances.

The best practices and lessons that we can learn will apply to *any* company, no matter how big or small. It will apply equally to the vendor that has a shop of five people and the vendor that has an operation of 250 people. I been fortunate in the my career to be part of both; part of a startup with a handful of people that grew to over 100 people, and part of two of the largest training outsource providers in our industry right now. My clients have included smaller, niche organizations like Krispy Kreme, and massive organizations like Microsoft and Bank of America. I mentioned some of my past clients in the Preface. I have seen examples in all shapes and sizes. What I have identified is that the Seven Attributes maps very cleanly to all of them.

Chapter 1

Current State

Habitually, every training department within a company has its own way of doing business. Often, many training professionals within a company have their own way of doing business. Within even in the largest training outsourcing providers, I've seen that each group has its own way of doing business. As a result, there is incredible inconsistency. Some of the training being produced is outstanding. Some of it is ridiculously boring or downright ugly. Some business initiatives are highly successful, and the training plays a strong part. Other business initiatives are delayed as a result of the training not being ready in time for the rollout. We've all seen this.

One of my most satisfying client engagements involved a very large product rollout. Our client was the largest company in its technology sector, by far. Chances are good that, if you've ever used a computer, you used one of their products. Back in 2006, I received a phone call from this company. At the time, it was early in our relationship and we had done only a little work for them—pockets of courses within human resources and product development, but nothing within the sales and marketing space.

So on that lucky day, my phone rang. On the other line was the head of the training department within sales and marketing who was in charge of rolling out the two largest product introductions in the history of their company. They had hired two vendors six months prior to develop the training—one that would focus on the content and the other that would focus on the technical requirements. The technical requirements in this case were bit hairy because there were 32 different roles involved in the rollout of the products; for example, the sales rep, the account manager, technical specialist, everyone involved with the introduction to the customer needed something a little bit different from the course.

On this phone call, she informed me that these two vendors were failing and that they had just informed her that they would not be able to hit their deadline. Training rollout was mandated by the Vice President of Sales Operations for August 1, only eight weeks away. This was a massive problem for them because the vice president had promised the tens of thousands of sales reps they would receive the training before the product was rolling out. Failure was not an option. She said very clearly, and an entrepreneur loves to hear these words: "Bill, I don't care how much this is going to cost, can you get it done on time?"

Of course, I said "yes," and then I pulled my team together to figure out how. The story continues and I'll tell you more about that later in the book, but the bottom line is this: They were facing two massive vendor failures that almost caused a catastrophic failure for business.

Ironically, this was the second time I'd received such a phone call. The first was from a top five pharmaceutical company. It was a similar scenario: a huge mandate as a result of a government regulatory settlement. The vendor they hired failed, 60 days remained on the time line, and the customer said: "Bill, I don't' care what it will cost, can you get it done on time?"

We succeeded on both missions. After the completion of the sales and marketing project, the message that we got with the final approval was worded simply, "Thank you for saving our jobs."

EVERY MAN FOR HIMSELF

The culprit is the lack of standards of practice. Anyone who ever taught a class and knows how to use PowerPoint can regard himself as an "instructional designer." Any individual working for herself or with a couple of mates can refer to herself as a "training development company." Who's to stop them? There is no blueprint for how to get our work done, how we should project manage, how we divide up the workflow, how we work with the subject matter experts, how we test our courses, and so on. So there is no consistency or predictability.

You may hire an individual who calls himself or herself an instructional designer and expect that person to produce great solutions, but you really don't know what you'll end up with. Those were very broad statements, and obviously in due

28

diligence, you may have some expectations based on their previous work. Granted, some companies out there do an exceptional job. I've been both a provider and had clients that were each exceptionally well organized and consistently produced great work. They do exist, but they are not the norm. The failure rate within training development outsourcing is extremely high. So this puts your typical company with your typical training organization in a scary situation. How do you pick the right provider?

There's a tremendous amount of expectation on the training departments nowadays. The budget is thin, the staffing is thin, and the business needs often come without warning. We don't have much time to get our work done, and we most certainly don't have the time to do it twice.

Chapter 2

Outsourcing

This is the era of outsourcing. Like it or not, it is a strategic imperative to remain competitive and respond to the increasing need to control costs. Whether you are contracting a single development project or your entire development operations, you must ensure that your vendor is capable of the challenge. But what should you look for? How do you spot it before the relationship begins?

The commitment to outsourcing bears risk. If you don't pick the right partner, then your reputation could be questioned and the success of your company could be challenged. You may not get a second chance to get it right. So how do you spot the vendor's weaknesses? How do you know if they will align with your organization?

Training development is complex. Let's assume that if the subject area was simple, you wouldn't need training. To design, develop, and implement an effective training program, you need to decipher the subject matter and then determine what the audience needs, the best instructional modality, the best instructional design strategy, how to get the subject matter from the heads of the SMEs, how to manage the review process, how to coordinate the online or media development, how to get it done on time and on budget, etc. There's nothing easy about it.

It's hard for you, and you work inside your company. It's harder for a vendor because they do not. So how do you know which vendors have the chops to do it right?

Unfortunately, there is no benchmark. The industry does not have an effective roadmap for success. There has never been a base metric that every procurement officer could reference to make the right decisions. This is not like outsourcing manufacturing or customer service, where this is a clear set of standards to draw upon and transactions to measure success. This is not like outsourcing accounting or legal, with industry-required educational and certification requirements. There are no standard for "good" learning. So what are the benchmarks for success? What standards should you seek? What processes work better than others?

In any business, you don't often get a second chance. A bad selection can be very costly because business is disrupted. Without effective training, product doesn't roll out on time, the sales force isn't prepared, compliance rules are violated, new employees are not trained to do their jobs, systems don't roll out on schedule, major projects and changes are not implemented, and the list goes on. The shake-out of a bad outsourcing relationship often involves the personal risk to the careers of those who made the selection.

Training development is ridiculously important to corporate success. Every major initiative and business function requires effective training. The speed of business demands that these training programs are developed swiftly and are available when these initiatives are ready.

Many development vendors have succeeded by applying efficient and effective techniques and producing outstanding results, while others fail by their inability to conceive and deploy an effective operation to meet their client's needs. Throughout this book, you'll hear many of these stories. I'll share many case studies of successes and failures, and how to avoid those failures in your future outsourcing.

In the end, I haven't seen it all, but I've seen so much. My viewpoint is shaped by the successes and failures I've witnessed. As I outline the Seven Attributes, I will use actual cases to illustrate the importance and best practices of each—both positive and negative.

SUCCESS

You turn to development partners/vendors because you want to tap into their expertise, supplement your own team, and produce an effective product (at a reasonable price). To do so, you spend time identifying likely candidates, preparing RFIs and RFPs, answering questions, reviewing results, negotiating pricing, and so on. You've invested lots of time and energy to find a partner.

So if everyone invests so much time, why is the success rate so low? Success or failure may result from personnel, process, and/or technology issues, as well as overselling and broken promises. How do you spot this up front? In this book, I hope to answer these questions and give you a strong blueprint for future success.

Let's start with my base premise: A successful outsourcing relationship is **"the equilibrium when the client is fully achieving their vision and the vendor is making a profit."** Both sides of this equation are important to success.

Let's think about why companies outsource. Typically, it is to reduce costs, increase quality, increase speed or efficiency, or tap into innovation (to name some common ones). If they are outsourcing the development of one course or responding to the layoff of the entire staff of training professionals, the goals are often still the same. They have needs, and they trust their "partner" to help them fulfill their needs and to do so in a manner that produces a positive return on investment.

Let's look at the vendor. The vendor must make a profit to stay in business. The client desires to push costs down as much as possible, but they must ensure that this does not prevent the vendor from making a profit. What happens when the vendor is losing money or (more commonly) is making less of a profit with your company than they may make with another client?

Several things may occur: They stop considering you as a priority, the staff assigned get frustrated due to limited budgets, the "partner" becomes a "vendor" and starts using terms like "off the rate card" or discussing the renegotiation of the contract rate table, and the more talented staff get assigned to other clients. The client must make sure that their account is "competitive" so they receive the best talent the vendor has to offer. In short, the vendor needs to earn a profit to maintain a healthy business and a healthy partnership with its clients.

This isn't a tricky equation. When the equation is balanced, great things happen. The product rolls out on time, the learners are pleased with the result, challenging business problems are solved with confidence, and the relationship continues to strengthen. When the equation is out of balance, no one is happy. The products take too long, the SMEs don't commit, the learners find the courses irrelevant, trust waivers, and too much time and energy is spent trying to salvage the relationship.

WHY SOME FAIL WHILE OTHERS SUCCEED

As I introduced earlier in this book, I set out to determine what made a successful outsourcing relationship, what made so many such relationships fail, and how to provide guidance for future success. It was important to me that all this guidance was tangible and applicable. We all understand that attributes like "trust" and "passion" are important, but it is vital that the Seven

Attributes focus on those areas where you have total control. At Option Six, "trust" was the first word on our website. It was the heart of what we provided, but it was achievable because we got the job done and our clients enjoyed our relationship.

Some preliminary assumptions regarding these attributes include:

- Defining a manageable number of attributes that matter most
- A focus on the day-to-day experience working with the vendor
- Assessment of the maturity of the development vendor's operations
- Consideration of fulfilling the "promises" presented during sales
- Treating the vendors fairly, not applying an unrealistic benchmark
- Balancing objectives based on quality and performance, not just size or cost

So what are the Seven Attributes? I summarize below. The remainder of the book is dedicated to the detail exploration of each attribute. In very simple terms and "in order of importance," the Seven Attributes are:

> **Experience:** The experience of the vendor related to the client's needs—the company and the actual people that they will assign, the quality of their past work, and the model for the day-to-day working relationship that will produce an effective outsourcing experience.

Methodology: The vendor's ownership of and dedication to an effective instructional design philosophy and methodology and their ability to apply it to a wide range of solutions types (low-level, high-level, one-off's, mass production, and all the latest modalities).

Infrastructure: The vendor's ability to sustain a scalable staffing model without sacrificing quality, their hiring and orientation processes, structure of the organization (centralized or decentralized), and the supporting operating structure.

Process: The workflows used to develop the training, including content drafting, reviews and testing, product development, SME interaction, the maturity and flexibility of their processes, team composition, and global integration.

Technology: The tools used to support the end-to-end development, including project management, resource management, reviews and testing, issues tracking, and workflow management, as well as experience with the client's tools.

Talent: The qualifications of the staff, including the education and experience, on-boarding and development programs, definition and assignment of roles, location, and on-going staff development.

Innovation: The vendor's ability to provide leadership in the adoption of new techniques and technologies, their involvement in the industry, proven success with adoption, and capability for experimentation.

Why in this order? If talent is so important, then why is it Attribute number six? Answer: There is a clear dependence between the Attributes. Without a strong predecessor, each attribute is weakened. For example, if the vendor has no experience in your business, then they are more likely to fail to understand your needs. You could have the brightest talent in the world, but if they are not supported by adequate infrastructure, processes, and technology, then they flounder with inconsistent results and will not achieve their potential. If the company doesn't have a solid methodology, then no matter how defined their development process, there is no assurance that the product will be "effective." Innovation is great, but not if you can't deliver the basic. And so on. These are some of the reasons why they are listed in this order.

What about price? Price is not one of the Seven Attributes. Price is part of doing business, but not an influencing factor in the day-to-day relationship. Providers will give you their best price. They all want your business. If you like the provider, but don't like the price, then negotiate. If a provider is charging significantly more than the others, contact them and find out why. They may be doing something substantially different, something you may want to consider, at least in part. Or they may misunderstand your scope. Never rule out the provider who best matches to your needs, along all Seven Attributes, simply because of price. It will cost you much more in the long run. **Remember, you are entrusting them with your business and your reputation (personal and company).** You don't get a chance to do this twice, not without more costs, and some of your training initiatives have no room for failure. You can blow out all the anticipated savings of a cheaper vendor very quickly with poor performance.

Remember, your vendor must make a profit. If they do not make a profit, your business will cease to be interesting to them and they will focus on other clients where they are making a profit; more likely, they will start talking about renegotiating very soon after the contract is signed.

Another way to define the Seven Attributes is to examine the type of questions that you may ask in an RFP that support (uncover) the important provider characteristics that will make the relationship successful. Here are some of these questions to consider.

Experience

- Will this relationship provide synergy for mutual benefit? Or is it simply another sales opportunity for the vendor?
- Does the vendor have experience in your industry and your needs?
- Does the vendor have experience with the levels of complexity required within your courseware or the complexity of your business needs?
- What is the vendor's approach to SME relationships? How do they plan to form a partnership with the SME (versus using carrots and sticks)?

- How will they align their management with yours? What are the qualifications of the planned account manager?
- Have they shown you the quality of their work through demos and cases? Have they shown you a typical day-to-day course (that you can afford), or only their award winners?
- Have they ever been fired? Why?
- Do you need to settle on just one vendor? Should you distribute the volume between multiple vendors? Should you retain a couple expert boutiques for specialty projects?

Methodology

- Do they have a methodology? Is it more than a re-titling of ADDIE (the five prongs of the instructional design model: analysis, design, development, implementation, evaluation)? Is it institutionalized or only a marketing asset? Does their methodology include only project administration tasks, or does it include instructional design and course development tasks?
- Do they have an instructional design philosophy and associated design strategy that complements the methodology?
- Do they have the ability to implement the methodology consistently across all course development? Is their staff well educated in the methods?
- Can their methodology be applied to different levels of complexity (L100-L400)? Can it be applied to different solutions (ILT, WBT, mobile, and so on)?

Can it be applied to various sized engagements: solo-course versus mass-scale development?

Infrastructure

- Do they have a sustainable staffing model? Can they scale (quickly) without sacrificing quality?
- Do they maintain a healthy utilization level and maintain a (reasonable) bench of available staff? Do they have the staff that you need now?
- Do they have a proactive recruiting process that provides a stable of available candidates? Or do they use JIT staffing after the projects are sold?
- What are the qualifications and experience (as an employee of the vendor) for each level of management assigned to the account?
- Do their financial processes align with yours? Are there ways to structure the statement of work and invoicing process to benefit both parties?
- Does their sales commission structure support long-term involvement with the relationship, or just the initial sales gains?

Process

- Do they use a waterfall approach or an iterative development process (such as AGILE)?
- Do they develop their online courseware (web-based, mobile, and so on) in an online environment or on paper-based storyboards?

- What is their drafting and review processes? Are they SME-friendly; do they utilize processes that are conducive to the SME's time availability?
- Do they enable online reviews of the online courseware while it is under development?
- Do they do user testing? Are the Alpha, Beta, and/or Pilot reviews of online courseware in an online environment for users, or are they paper-based SME reviews?
- Do they provide for flexibility in the process and timelines, given that everyone is busy, time commitments vary, and priorities often change? How does their process adapt to these changes?
- What roles are involved in the process? Do they use one core ID to do all the design and development, or do they employ a team of multiple staff with different roles/expertise?
- How do they integrate their offshore staff (if used)? Do they offshore specific tasks, the whole project, or does it vary? What review process do they use for offshore work?

Technology

- What technology do they have in place to manage their workflow: work assignment, file management, review management, issues tracking, comment tracking, etc.?
- What tools do they use for project management? Do they have a system other than MS Project or spreadsheets? Is it tied to their financial systems? How much of the budget of each project is used for project management?

- What technology do they use for course testing and issues tracking/resolution?
- What experience do they have with your toolset?

Talent

- What are their qualifications? Do they have master's degrees or bachelor's degrees? Do they have experience developing training or just managing it?
- Does the staff assigned have experience handling the complexity of the business needs (subject matter) you will assign to them?
- Do they have an effective on-boarding program? Do the new employees receive training on their methodology and work processes?
- If they are centralized, do they have a mentorship program? If they are decentralized, how do they support the growth and performance of their employees?
- Do they use all-in-one instructional designers (with the possible exception of media production), or do they use teams of multiple people focused on specific roles?
- How do they support the on-going staff development? Do they have social learning programs? How do they share best practices across accounts?
- Are they a consulting company or a staffing company? Which does your company need?

Innovation

- Do they have experience in the emerging technologies and techniques?

- Do they have a team of and reputation as thought-leaders? Do they have more than one thought-leader?
- Are they involved in the industry? Do they speak at conferences or publish?
- Do they have the internal infrastructure to test and experiment with new innovations? Can they help you adopt new ideas and tools?

I have been fortunate to be involved with so many successful outsourcing initiatives. I've also been fortunate to witness the large number of failures that are occurring. From both sides, I've garnered the direction and advice that will certainly improve your odds of a successful outsourcing relationship. I further hope that, while the Seven Attributes are written o guide the client to making better selections, they may also provide guidance to outsource providers who want to improve their level of services and increase their competitive ability.

Chapter 3

Attribute #1: Experience

What do a boat captain and an account manager have in common? No matter how refined your plan is, if you pick the wrong one you may not end up (safely) at your intended destination. In fact, an incompetent captain or account manager could send the entire journey to catastrophic failure, no matter how good the crew is.

Imagine for a moment that you have a development partner. Their lead—perhaps called an Account Manager, Course Director, or something to that effect—is available to you whenever you need him/her. They understand your situation, your industry, the type of learning programs you are building, and they are a great sounding board for your vision. They enjoy bouncing around ideas, giving insight, challenging you, and providing the reality checks needed. In short, "they get it."

Over time, you've learned to trust this partner. They bring great people to the projects, are enjoyable to work with, and produce great results. Sure, it's not always perfect. Things happen that can affect any aspect of the project, but the *trust* is there and you're always able to resolve the issue and move on successfully.

Wouldn't that be nice? Unfortunately, as many of you know, this is not always the case. In fact, there is a solid reason why Experience is #1 in the Seven Attributes. If this attribute fails, then nothing else really matters. Even if the product being produced is acceptable, it's just a matter of time before someone "easier to work with" comes along.

One of my favorite clients was the engineering division of an exceptionally large technology company; in fact, they are the largest in their industry, by a long shot. We were introduced when this client issued an RFP to find one or more vendors for their custom course development. We were fortunate enough to be invited to bid on it. We won and were awarded half of their portfolio. Another firm was awarded the other half. This is a common practice, not putting all your eggs in one basket, as they say. Within six months, the client began assigning many of the other vendor's courses to us. Within the year, we were doing all the work. Why? Our working relationship, the trust, and the quality of the result were some reasons, but that wasn't the total reason. The client stated quite firmly, "Our SMEs don't like working with the other vendor."

TRUST

You have to trust your outsourcing partner with your business. You *need* to trust them. There is a reason you are outsourcing: quality, expertise, volume, efficiency, innovation, or cost. Your reason doesn't matter. You need a partner who can fulfill your needs. You made a strategically important decision to outsource, no matter whether it's a single course or the training development for your whole organization. Regardless, if the relationship fails, then lots of people are not happy. That includes you, your supervisors, your stakeholders, the business functions relying on your service, your SMEs, your learner, and so on. The training programs that are "nice to have" are rapidly being eliminated due to downward financial pressures. The only programs remaining are "the really important ones," and you rarely get a second chance to get it right.

So, there are lots of expectations to identify a vendor with the right experience. You're handing them lots of responsibility. If they are successful, everyone is happy. If they are not, no one is happy.

Let me give you an example. (To protect the reputation of the vendor and client, I'll withhold any identifiable information.)

I was recently asked to help salvage a bad relationship between a provider and their client. Actually, the client's CLO made the direct request for me to help via text messages during a disastrous project review meeting. When he called me, he simply stated, "We've lost all confidence in [the vendor]."

The client is a technology company; in fact, the biggest in their industry (though a different technology company than the one I introduced above). If you are using a computer of any type, chances are good that it includes one of their products. The vendor is also one of the largest providers in their industry. The vendor company has been around for decades and, as a company, has a tremendous brand in the area of training. So the marriage seemed ideal. The client chose the vendor because of their reputation, *touted* experience, size and strength, global reach, etc.

This is where the definition of the "experience" attribute is so important. On paper, in the sales proposal, this looked like a good fit, until the vendor assigned the team. What the two parties did not align during the sales process, either through lack of knowledge or overselling, was the experience in the subject areas the client needed and the experience of the people who would be assigned.

Now, you might assume that a technology company's training needs would tend to be fairly standard. As long as you stay away from the engineering professions, the needs within human resources, marketing, sales, and so on may be much like any other company. At the time, they simply referred to the targeted domain as "non-technical," but in this particular case, the needs were in the areas of corporate culture and leadership. In fact, some of the leadership topics dealt with heavyweight topics like strategy and interpersonal dynamics. Those are challenging topics: intangible, specialized, multiple perspectives, and often requiring third-party experts. To be successful, this would require a team with some pretty unique skills and experiences.

The issue started when the provider assigned a team that had no experience in those domains. In fact, the account manager assigned had never led a training development account. His/her background was in training administration and had recently worked with a client who fired the vendor. So while the experience of the company appeared to align with the client's needs, on paper, the experience of the actual team being assigned did not align.

Now, the issues with this relationship ran deep and spanned across many of the Seven Attributes, but in this case, the <u>experience</u> of the provider was the problem, not simply the experience of the provider's company. Remember, they had a strong brand. Rather, it was the experience of the people from that company. Of the thousands of employees in the provider's company, they picked the wrong six. That wasn't fair to the client, or fair to the team who were put in a position where failure was likely.

After consulting with the CLO, we replaced the full team, top to bottom, with a team that had the right experiences and the results were seen instantly, in both the quality of the work and the strength of the relationship.

Could this have been avoided in the RFP process? Certainly! Although it is very challenging for the provider to provide the resumes of everyone who may be staffed to the account— keeping in mind that providers don't typically have their star players sitting around waiting for a new client and you haven't awarded the work yet—they certainly could have provided the bio of the account manager and other senior staff. In fact, it's not uncommon to request an interview with the account manager, even request that they attend the formal presentation (if there is one). This is the one area where you cannot afford to make a mistake. Personally, I always bring the lead resource with me to every sales meeting or proposal presentation. This is an arranged marriage. The chemistry must be there for it to work. Both the client and my leader must tell me that this will be a good fit.

And it is okay to ask the vendor if they, or the leaders that they are assigning, have ever been fired from an account and/or interview the last client they had. It might seem obvious to state that your chosen vendor must have "experience," but what type of experience? Should you expect them to have many years of experience in your industry? Experience within your function: leadership, accounting, manufacturing, compliance, or marketing? Should they have experience with your chosen and planned modalities: online, mobile, social, and so on? For the ideal partner in training development, I imagine that you'd look for a company that had all of these, and hope that they were the lowest bidder. Wouldn't that be nice?

WHAT MATTERS MOST?

If I were about to produce a series of courses to help my company to, for example, transition their brand on a global basis, I'd look for a development partner that had experience with <u>marketing</u> subjects, <u>complex</u> solutions because the topic of branding is challenging to understand and even harder to teach, <u>global</u> audience because culture is a big consideration, probably e-<u>learning</u> because the most efficient delivery method would be online, and I may be working with a <u>third party</u> to define our branding strategy, so it'd be nice to have a partner with that type of experience. With a highly successful RFP process, I should be able to find this company to provide a development team with each of these experiences. That sounds like the right assessment of experience in this case.

One final note: When they show you their sample work, does it reflect work that any of their teams could produce, or only the award winners? What will your *everyday* solutions look like? I once assisted an outsourcing provider in a presentation. I was speaking on the topic of blended solutions and the impact of new social learning technologies. They were highlighting innovation solutions from their company. After the presentation, I inquired about the demos that they showed. They were produced for several of their clients, and each had used some intriguing techniques. I contacted the account manager from each client, and *in every case,* this vendor did not produce the course. They were each produced by a third-party, subcontracted by the vendor. So when it comes to interviewing your vendor, be sure that what the vendor is showing you is something that they truly are capable of producing.

A DAY IN THE LIFE (AND WHAT ABOUT SME)

What will the working experience be like with this partner? You are going to be working with this vendor almost daily, and most likely you will assign them projects that are very important to your career. The working experience with the vendor's employees is paramount to success.

At the account level, who will you be working with? Who will be interrelating with your superiors, the vendor's superiors? For large accounts, it is common to have multiple levels of account management and communications: overall account, business units, projects, etc. At the highest level, this refers to the operations of the account and how work gets done. At a granular level, the most important working experience is between the provider's project team, your team, and subject matter experts.

Now, this is where the real success or failures occur. Of the hundreds of projects that my teams have executed, the relationship with the SME is very often the critical factor in success or failure. Therefore, in the proposal process, and then in the operationalization process after the award, establishing the vendor's experience working with SMEs and the processes that they will follow is a key criteria.

There are a variety of methods to establishing a good SME relationship. Using *carrots and sticks* is not one of them. In 2012, I participated in a research study with TrainingIndustry.com that determined the strategies that had worked best. Incentives like financial bonuses or including their name in the course credits did not increase the SME's ability/willingness to participate actively in the project. Penalties, *telling on them* to their manager, also produced very little benefit. Here's the issue. The reason that they are the subject matter "experts" is because they are the most knowledgeable and highest performing employees. Thus, **they are busy,** and the demands on their time are substantial.

The research findings suggest that there are several <u>effective</u> strategies to forming an effective SME partnership. First, they need to feel part of the project—not just a transactional relationship where you send them email requests and expect "great" responses, drafts, materials in return. Likewise, this relationship cannot be formed with all-day planning sessions at the beginning and all-day review sessions at the end. The relationship cannot be formed with intermediaries, such as client-side instructional designers, filtering the relationship. We all understand that the SMEs do not want to be pestered or have their time wasted, but they are a critical part of the project, so they must be actively involved.

So how do you involve them? You must adapt to their working style. They do not have four concentrated hours to review your storyboards. They do not have a full day to sit in a room and listen to you read the scripts. And, most of all, your chances are very slim of "getting it right" on the first draft you show them—unless you are developing a manufacturing course and have approved, inalterable, SOPs as your source. You most certainly would not achieve this assumption with a leadership course, marketing course, compliance, sales, etc. Why? **Because you don't understand their business as well as a SME**, so why would you think you could understand how the content is used in the business as well as the SME?

What do you do to involve the SME, and do so in a manner that works within their work style? Answer: a little at a time. The SME doesn't have huge concentrations of time to write or review the content; none of us do. You must provide *your* drafts and request *their* drafts, in small chucks. These are easily digestible, quick-to-respond exchanges that fit within their natural working style. "Please send us an example of when the compliance rule affects a sales rep." "Please review the attached scenario. Is it accurate? Is it relevant?" These are digestible exchanges that will get the SME actively, continuously involved and provide you the essential information you need.

Unfortunately, the prevailing practice is to set up as many hurdles as possible to protect the SME's time, reserving the reviews and working sessions to singular events. The research findings showed that this strategy doesn't help. My personal observations are that it is inefficient, inconvenient, and ineffective. Instead of working sessions three times during the project, or half-day review periods once per week, I'd suggest short exchanges every day. Blasphemy! This works within the natural work habits of SMEs and most of us. We produce and respond to information continuously throughout the day. SMEs can provide you as much information as they have at the beginning of the project, but the massaging, contextualizing, and completion of the information is the most important part, and where *constant refinement* is a better strategy.

We use the adage "get it wrong as fast as possible," so we can focus on getting it right. We all acknowledge that it is easier to edit than to create; thus, it is easier for SMEs to respond to something already created than it is to write something from scratch. The most important requirement for making this work is your own diligence. First, like it or not, **you must learn the subject matter**. You may not become an expert, but you must learn the subject well enough to ask intelligent questions and interpret information. In many ways, by the end of the project, you must be able to perform as well as the students taking the course. Second, **your work must be meticulous**. If the SME provides you information or feedback on a draft, and then must fix the same information or provide the same feedback on the second review, they will *indeed* believe that they are wasting their time. Make sure you have a disciplined comment-tracking process to avoid silly items from *falling through the cracks* and distracting from the substantive items that you hope to address. (See the Technology attribute for more about comment-tracking tools.)

ONE IS A LONELY NUMBER

When it comes to finding the right experience, you don't have to choose just one vendor. When a company has decided to outsource a large segment of their training organization, perhaps a full division or the entire company, often the goals are to consolidate the array of small providers, produce consistency across the products, build efficiency, save money, and tap innovation, among other needs.

In the training industry, a handful of companies are positioned for these major initiatives, in terms of having the perceived access to resources and the ability to scale to the client's needs. (There will be more on this perception in the Infrastructure section.) However, the large providers, while they are positioned to handle high volumes, they are not always the best choice for the ad-hoc, one-off projects, or those that are addressing higher level, mission critical, and/or complex skill sets. There is often a gap in capability. In contrast, the smaller boutiques are often very good at these small initiatives, yet do not have the ability to scale to the large demands (nor may they want to). This isn't a perfect example. Many of the larger providers may argue that they can do *everything and anything* asked of them, but I've not seen a case where this is true.

Let me use this example: A very large pharmaceutical company outsourced their entire company's training development to one of the larger providers. However, they still use a smaller boutique firm for all their product sales courses. Why? Because those courses are very specialized and highly sensitive, and **there's no room for error**. Prior to sole sourcing the training development, the client had a very successful relationship with this boutique firm and (very wisely) decided that they would not risk it. Any delay in the release of the associated training would cause a delay in the release of a new product. This particular pharmaceutical company loses $1M a day when they are not selling their new product. The boutique charges substantially more than the sole source provider, but the client pays the larger fee because they sleep well at night knowing that the projects will be successful, product will roll out on time, and everyone will be happy.

In another example, a large provider has a development agreement with one of the largest technology companies. They developed many HR courses for the technology company. However, the client used a boutique firm for their leadership courses. Why? This smaller firm has a unique expertise in the area of leadership, with a specialized simulation that they use in their courses. In this case, to simplify the administrative processes for the client, the boutique subcontracts through the larger provider. (By the way, if you value your boutique provider, I would not suggest this. The larger providers have longer payment terms, as the clients often have long payment terms. Thus, the smaller provider—the one where every dollar counts—gets penalized with a later payment from the sole provider than if they contracted directly with the client. I've seen this time and again: The small provider is nearly finished with the full project before seeing the first dollar of income.)

If you had a cold, you wouldn't go see an oncologist. If you had cancer, you wouldn't rely on your general practitioner. Just because a hospital has a great reputation doesn't mean that they have the best maternal program. The best method to ensure success is to choose the partner with the right experience, both within the company and the people you will be working with day to day. One size fits all isn't always the best answer, so keep some of your best boutiques on hand. Just like medicine, sometimes you need a specialist.

WHAT IS THEIR MOTIVE?

One of the more important assessments in the Experience attribute is *why* the vendor wants your business. Is it just the revenue and ability to add your logo to their portfolio, or does your company fit strategically into their business? For example, one of the largest providers in the training space, one who has seen many successes in the automotive, pharmaceutical, and transportation industries, was assessing an RFP from a university who was planning to launch a new online curriculum. The opportunity was attractive—tens of millions over multiple years. However, the provider did not have experience in academia. At the end of the day, they decided not to bid on the project. Although it is rare that the provider pulls away from an opportunity, the provider's experience in academia certainly has been something that the prospective client should have assessed.

I have been party to multiple occurrences where a provider planned to bid on an RFP, scoured their company looking for *any* past projects that were relevant, and proceeded to bid regardless of how little experience the company had (or their available staff had) toward that subject area or industry. You can only imagine what the client experience is like during the projects if they are awarded to a provider with no experience in the industry, subject matter, or ability to assign staff with that experience. Recall the non-technical curriculum provider from my early example? I can't recall how many times I've been party to a proposal process where a provider is moving full force to submit a bid, while simultaneously interviewing someone to lead it. That's a scary situation to be caught in, no matter which side of the fence you work on.

On the contrary, I have been party to several providers who *pursue* opportunities that are aligned with their strategy and *avoid* those that are <u>not</u>, no matter how attractive. One of my larger accounts was in the financial industry. When the RFP arrived, two facts were in our favor. First, the volume of work was huge and the client would be outsourcing entire divisions of work; we had demonstrated success with similar accounts. Second, we had experiences in the finance industry—not lots of experience and not at this magnitude, but we felt that the combination of our experience with similar accounts, the specific subject areas (marketing and product sales), in addition to our scalability (refer to Infrastructure) positioned us to be a successful partner. In the end, we won the account and were able to establish a very successful relationship.

What we did following this win is the most relevant story. The company determined that they would commit to the finance industry. They built off this recent success to pursue other opportunities specific to the finance industry, and in the end is one of the leaders; in fact, they are possibly the *de facto* choice in the finance industry. I witnessed them compete on a banking RFP against several other large providers and the boutique incumbent, who were all fighting hard to produce the best proposal and sales pitch. This provider I've referenced here merely carried one theme, "We've done this before. We've done it for clients just like you, and we've done it successfully. Here, call our clients." It's hard to beat that.

If you were the prospective client, and you were assessing the responses to the RFP, a provider experience in your industry would be foremost on your mind, but a vendor's *dedication* to your industry would be an even more interesting value point. "We've done this before and we did it successfully" is the best sales pitch you could hear.

In another example, a boutique company with only 30 employees bid on an RFP for one of the largest technology companies in the world. They bid against larger boutiques, two of the industry's largest providers, and one of the Big Four consulting firms. The smaller boutique firm won. How? First, they had recently been very successful in another division of that company, so they demonstrated that they had the chops to be successful in this company. Second, they planned to assign the *same team* that worked on that other project. That was a big factor also. The client stated, "I'm taking a chance on your company, but I like your people." In the end, the project was a big success and won an international award. This highlights the first definition of the Experience attribute: the experience of the people who will be assigned. While the other bidders were very respected companies, the client did not yet know or trust their employees.

So success breeds success—as it should. The clients should pick vendors who have been successful, and when a vendor finds a niche where they can be successful, they should place a strong focus on that niche. Vendors who see opportunities that fall outside their past experience should either <u>avoid</u> them or come up with an alternative approach, such as a partnership with another company with that domain expertise, before bidding on the campaign.

WHAT ABOUT PRICE?

I'll talk about price often. Price is not one of the Seven Attributes. Why? Because it has no bearing on the success of the relationship. It doesn't matter how cheap the provider is; if they don't have the experience, then your initiative will fail. Price can produce one of two negative side effects. First, you may select the wrong vendor because they are simply the lowest bidder and produced a great *looking* proposal, but don't really have the right experience. This is a recipe for failure because the low price leaves no room for error. Second, you may overlook a vendor who has a perfect alignment with a high probability of success, but is priced higher than the competition. My advice is to identify the best vendor along the Seven Attributes, **then negotiate.** There are probably some very good reasons why they are more expensive, and in our field, you get what you pay for.

There are many ways to align a working relationship within an outsourcing engagement. The boxes and arrows in the proposal may look great, but it's the experience of the people in those boxes that will, in the end, determine your success.

THE FINAL QUESTION

To summarize, here are the key questions that you are trying to answer in the Experience attribute:

- Will this relationship provide synergy for mutual benefit? Or is it simply another sales opportunity for the vendor?
- Does the vendor have experience in your industry and your needs?
- Does the vendor have experience with the levels of complexity required within your courseware or the complexity of your business needs?
- What is the vendor's approach to SME relationships? How do they plan to form a partnership with the SME (versus using carrots and sticks)?
- How will they align their management with yours? What are the qualifications of the planned account manager?
- Have they shown you the quality of their work through demos and cases? Have they shown you a typical day-to-day course (that you can afford), or only their award winners?
- Have they ever been fired? Why?

- Do you need to settle on just one vendor? Should you distribute the volume between multiple vendors? Should you retain a couple expert boutiques for specialty projects?

Chapter 4

Attribute #2: Methodology

What do an accountant and an instructional designer have in common? Nothing! An accountant has a firm academic requirement, a certification test to pass, and standard protocols and processes that must be observed when performing their job. An instructional designer has none of these. When you need to assess the experience of your development partner, you need well-structured criteria because, unlike accounting and many other formal practices, there is no standard for evaluating the experience of training development partners.

Imagine for a moment that you have been in this industry for a while, either as a consultant that has been developing training, or the leader of a training organization, or even just a learner attending online and classroom programs. Imagine that you have had very positive experiences with some courses and that you feel those courses were extremely effective. Wouldn't it be fantastic if every course developed engendered that same feeling?

What if every training development team, every instructional designer, was able to produce a training program—a learning experience—that was highly effective and highly engaging to the learner and simultaneously achieve the business objective of their stakeholders? As we've noted, there is no standard for the qualifications of an instructional designer, so their backgrounds are varied, but what if it were possible to produce consistent learning experiences, regardless of the instructional designer's background? Wouldn't it be utopia if you could create an environment where all this was true?

Foremost in this conversation, we must agree with the premise that an *accurate presentation of content* and *an effective instructional experience* are entirely different. Just because the content is correct and includes what the SME provided does not mean that the instruction is effective or that it includes what the learner needs to achieve the level of performance desired. (If you do not agree with this assessment, then kindly apologize to your learners and skip to the Process section.)

The strategy that the developers will follow to produce the best quality product is the #2 Attribute: Methodology. This is the method and techniques they will follow to craft the content (scope, sequence, breakdown, etc.), how they determine the best instructional approach (case study, problem based, etc.), the objectives (business, performance, learning, etc.), the usage of media, and so on. The Methodology attributes embodies these needs.

WHICH MODEL DO I CHOOSE?

Now, I do not pretend to be an instructional designer. I will outline the best practices and cases that I have witnessed. What I know has been garnered from the last 14 years working with really good instructional designers and witnessing really bad ones. I cannot design a course, but I can distinguish great, good, bad, and ugly.

There are popular models for instructional design in our industry, the most common of which is ADDIE (analysis, design, development, implementation, evaluation). It covers the obvious: Think about what you need to build, design it first, build it, install it, and keep an eye on it. I think we can all agree that those are pretty good ideas, although we all acknowledge that the "A" and "E" are often neglected. The problem with ADDIE is that it works great in a vacuum—one course with a thoroughly trained instructional designer—but that does not define today's corporate world. In our world, we have many projects simultaneously competing for a limited number of resources, a wide range of subject areas and modalities, and a wide range of capabilities in the staff developing them. ADDIE is simply not prescriptive enough, nor dynamic enough to handle the myriad of variances, to be used as the sole guide for training development. It outlines <u>what</u> needs to be done, but not the best way to do it.

Let's also distinguish between a methodology that is focused on *the integrity of the product* and one that focuses on *getting the work through the stages of development*. Oh, there is a big difference. The latter is focused on project management and the interrelations between functions within the team. I cover that within Attribute #4: Process. A methodology is different than a process. A process, even one that is highly effective, addresses the tasks, getting sign-offs, and finishing the work on time, but it does not guarantee that the product is successful. It doesn't ensure that the instructional design technique is effective for this subject matter and this audience. It doesn't ensure that the end result, the new level of performance, will accomplish the initial performance objective. That is where a solid methodology is required.

I've seen many companies take ADDIE and put their own spin on it. That's reasonable, but too often what I have witnessed is not an interpretation by the training team, but a recasting by the marketing team, with a new acronym and trademark to show off during sales. Overall, it doesn't matter what you call your methodology. What does matter is (a) whether it is sound and effective and (b) whether **all the developers in your company understand it and apply it consistently.**

I once interacted with a very large provider in the training industry. They promoted that they have a methodology. It has a slick acronym that reinterprets ADDIE, and there are four philosophical statements that describe the assumptions behind it. But that's where it ended. Other than the marketing group using it in proposals, no one else used it. They do not have a structured pedagogical approach to apply within the methodology, nor do they have an orientation program to teach the employees how to apply the methodology. Without these elements, you have a great looking diagram, but that's all. Without a solid, integrated methodology, everyone in their company—every consultant assigned to a different client—still built the courses based on their own experience, differently than everyone else with widely inconsistent results.

DON'T UNDERESTIMATE YOR COMPLEXITY

Without a methodology, it's *every man for himself.* Instructional design is complex. I'll admit that I had no clue what "instructional design" was when I started my career, and it was years before I fully understood how they saw the world differently. I've learned to respect the trade over the past decade, to the point where I won't go into a proposal presentation without an instructional designer by my side. Unfortunately, there is no standard in our industry for what qualifies a person to title himself an instructional designer. To paraphrase Andy

Warhol, "Anyone can be an instructional designer, but very few really are." Now, this randomness may be endured in a typical corporate setting. The corporate environment often provides an existing team and structure, provides a person time to learn what is needed and/or take additional education to fill in the gaps. Again, without a solid methodology, there is no guarantee that the person will successfully assimilate, but still may produce inadequate products.

However, if you are choosing a provider to produce your training, then **any randomness is unacceptable.** You ought to expect that a vendor's instructional designers have a solid grasp on the trade. You should expect that when a vendor assigns a team, the team has proven track record and have been thoroughly trained in their craft. You should expect that any and every course produced by that vendor has a consistent degree of quality and effectiveness.

Thus, it is essential that a training development vendor has a well-crafted, proven methodology— that there is a **philosophy and pedagogy** behind it, that it is tied to a prescriptive instructional model, and most of all, that every instructional designer has been trained on the methodology and can consistently and diligently apply it to every client and every project condition. Those are the vendors who have the highest likelihood of success.

One of the more effective providers I've seen had three components to their methodology: a process that they would follow (Attribute #4), a philosophy that guided the products that they produced, and a detailed pedagogy that reflected the instructional practices that they knew worked. Their process was detailed, and I'll revisit that in the Process section, but these latter two components were the most important. Every course produced would follow this philosophy and would apply the techniques within the pedagogy, consistently. In many ways, it provided a recipe for every employee to follow. It included not just techniques that would be effective, but also their overall *attitude* toward what makes an effective solution. They clearly defined what worked. Personally, when I talk about methodology, I like the term "philosophy" because there is a clear distinction from the *boxes and arrows*.

ASSESSING THE METHODOLOGY

The Methodology attribute can best be defined along these three dimensions. First, does the organization have one? Second, does it include enough detail to provide a solid blueprint to the instructional designer? Third, does everyone in the organization understand it and apply it?

There are many ways to create a methodology; what is most important is getting beyond the boxes and the arrows and funky acronyms, the re-titling of ADDIE, to produce something that truly guides the instructional designer through the process of, not only *efficiently* creating the training material, but also producing an <u>effective</u> learning experience—one that provides the employee with the skills they need to do their job and, when you really want to get sophisticated, a learning experience that provides the employees the skills they need to achieve the company's business objectives. That is the real goal.

One of the components of a solid methodology is how well it will hold up in different situations; one that may work exceptionally well for a single course may not work well in an environment that is trying to produce 100 courses. What might work for a standard compliance course, if there is such a thing, may not work well for a more complex leadership course. What works well for classroom training may not work well for online training or mobile training. The strength of a good methodology is that it will hold up in a wide range of circumstances.

I do not believe that there is only one way to implement a methodology. I won't say that there's only one methodology that works in our industry. I've seen some outstanding examples crafted by providers, and there are some exceptional methodologies available for purchase, such as the *Six Disciplines of Breakthrough Learning.* I think it is okay that different training organizations have an interpretation and have designed a methodology that works well within their environment. What works exceptionally well for a pharmaceutical company and a manufacturing company may differ greatly. What works well for marketing or engineering may be entirely different. That is okay.

The execution of a good methodology may take shape in a variety of forms. The standard format of training materials, the user interface of online courses, the way they go about doing their reviews and testing, the structure and style of the design document—these are all elements of the execution of a methodology that can vary. These can vary for a specific company, but **should not vary** from department to department and certainly not by individual. I do firmly believe that if you defined a methodology, and do it in such a way that you know it works in your environment, then that methodology should not change from person to person. Clearly, if there was one methodology we could all adopt, and always rely on, then I'd be all for it.

THE BIRTH OF A METHODOLOGY

When I started my development company back in 2001, I had a stellar cast of employees that I inherited from an organization that was developing online MBA programs. It's a great story, but

I won't bore you with it at this time. Nonetheless, with a new company, I thought it was very important for us to sit down and figure out what our methodology was going to be. If we were going to grow and hire more people, and I was going to assign these people to our clients, then I wanted to make sure they were all doing it in the same way; I didn't want to get phone calls because someone decided to be a rebel and apply techniques that were ineffective. So I assembled a group of our instructional designers and my senior staff to think this through.

We started where lots of people start. We started with the format and interface of our products. We asked, "What should our brand or standard be?" We very quickly realized that we were asking the wrong questions. Of course we wanted consistency within the look and feel of our courses, but we also realized that as a vendor, we would not be able to dictate the standards to our clients. We may love the color blue on our interface, but that doesn't mean the client would. No, it was most certainly not the interface or the format of the materials that would define our standards and our brand. Rather, it was **the way we approach every project.** It was the instructional design principles that we applied to every course. It was the overall philosophy that we held true as to what made truly effective training. In the end, that was the foundation of our methodology, not the boxes and arrows.

To define a methodology, we broke down the methodology into two dimensions: the instructional design philosophy and the pedagogy.

The methodology, in terms of the boxes and arrows, was actually quite primitive. It was a high-level conceptual diagram that fundamentally showed that we would plan the project, design the project, develop the project, and conclude the project. The processes were based on both ADDIE and the software development lifecycle (SDLC), an integration that is now commonly referred to as AGILE. As such, given that it's not an assembly line, the process did not require a great deal of segmentation. We did use a clever set of terms—Envision, Engage, Evaluate—but that's not the point.

The point is that we didn't spend a tremendous amount of time on the boxes and arrows.

Where we spent time was developing instruments that would allow our staff to produce excellent products. The instructional design philosophy, in this case six primary principles, guided every decision they made during the instructional design of a project. We had certain beliefs that all training programs should include these principles, such as being solution-oriented and context-driven, being learner-centered versus SME-centered, flexible, interactive, and so forth. Every single one of their courses had to be focused on solving a problem, had to provide a learner multiple ways of going through the training, and had to be focused on what the learner needed to know instead of what the subject matter expert wanted to teach them; that distinction absolutely confused me at first, but it became very clear after I saw it in practice. In short, it is the difference between training that is *accurate* versus training that's *effective*. We had very clearly defined each principle, embedded them into the DNA of the company, and designed the instruments around it that would enable every instructional designer to follow them.

The second component of our methodology was the pedagogy. In this case, it was a derivative of problem-based learning. Our primary business focus was custom corporate e-learning, so we determined that this was the best foundation for the type of business problems that we would be helping the client solve. Early in my career, my employer, Anderson Consulting, referred to it as performance-based design. There are many ways to title it. What we did that was of utmost importance was find a way to outline it in such detail that an instructional designer would be able to **apply** it consistently, and where there was **validity** behind the pedagogy. It wasn't simply created in-house, but in participation with several faculty members of highly rated instructional design programs, and even a couple exceptionally notable experts in usability in the industry. Then it was tested over and over and over and over again, over 10,000 hours (the benefits of an association with a highly funded dot-com in the late 1990s), <u>before</u> being uniformly applied throughout our company.

IS INSTRUCTIONAL DESIGN THE HARDEST JOB IN THE WORLD?

I believe that instructional design is a bit of an *art and science.* In this book, I often use the comparison between instructional design and something like accounting, but to be fair, accounting is governed by a set of rules and axioms, whereas an instructional designer is not so tangible. An ID must take a complex situation, an urgent business initiative, perhaps a subject they don't understand, possibly with a global audience of tens of thousands of employees, and turn that into a highly engaging and effective learning experience—and do so in less than 45 minutes. There's nothing simple about this at all, which is why I get on my soapbox and state that we must have standards for the education and experience level of the people tackling these projects and the processes and tools by which they are using to complete the work. This is why I insist on an implementation of methodology guided by a set of philosophies that have been turned into very specific style of training, using an instructional design strategy that has proven to be effective, and not just a linear presentation of what the subject matter expert told the instructional designer.

In 2011, I was fortunate to win an account with a very large financial institution. At that time, they were the largest financial institution in their industry sector. They may have also been the most scrutinized. There was nothing small or trivial about the business challenges they were facing. I have never been in an environment that had a greater sense of urgency. I was very impressed with this client because, before hiring any vendors, they spent a tremendous amount of time designing the structure of their learning organization, the processes they would follow to do work, and building a technical infrastructure that would help managed the large portfolio of projects. Once they had selected their vendors, they required that these vendors follow their methodology, use their tools, and keep their information up to date in the project management system. This was an impressive organization. While no organization is perfect, this was among the most successful, highest-performing environments and made the best use of development providers of any I've witnessed.

Now, obviously, much goes into developing a solution of this nature. It was very complex, very large, with lots of moving parts, but the bottom line is that every training department in the company was using the same processes, every vendor was using the same processes, all the materials looked the same—not simply the format of the instructor guides and online courses, but also the analysis and design documents and every interim deliverable, and they had a common technical infrastructure that the entire company could use to keep all the moving parts moving. All these things combined to produce a tremendously efficient operation. (In general, the training industry lacks an off-the-shelf solution of this nature, which is why I formed my current company, **Quantum7**, to finally provide one.)

As one of their providers, I also appreciated the flexibility that they provided that enabled us to integrate our processes, which had worked exceptionally well for us in the decade prior to this, with their processes. While they had standards, they were not dogmatic about it. They accepted that they had hired us because we were successful in the past and we were able to find a common ground.

This bears repeating. You probably selected your provider because you deemed that they were the best provider for your needs, and that their prior success had sufficiently prepared them and their operation was efficient and effective so that they could meet your timeline and budgetary needs. If all this is true, then the last thing you should do is force them to change all that. While you must implement a uniform environment your own organization, you must also leave room for synchronization with your provider.

One of the things that most terrifies the development leaders of the provider is when their sales people negotiate a price that is too low. I'll discuss these strategies in the pricing section. For this financial services client, it was the most aggressive pricing that I had worked under. Had it not been for that highly evolved infrastructure of our organization at the time, and the precisely designed infrastructure of <u>my client,</u> we could never have achieved success. Instead, we produced some outstanding materials that helped them realize the vision that they had for their outsourcing program and make a profit in the process, which I will say over and over again is fundamentally important to any training outsourcing initiative. The vendor must make a profit so they can stay in business and continue to provide excellent support to your organization.

THE FINAL QUESTION

To summarize, here are the key questions that you are trying to answer in the Methodology attribute:

- Do they have a methodology?
- Is it more than a re-titling of ADDIE?
- Is it institutionalized or only a marketing asset?
- Does their methodology include only project administration tasks, or does it include instructional design and course development tasks?
- Do they have an ID philosophy and associated design strategy that complements the methodology?

- Do they have the ability to implement the methodology consistently across all course development?
- Is their staff well educated in the methods?
- Can their methodology be applied to different levels of complexity (L100-L400)?
- Can it be applied to various sized engagements: solo-course versus mass-scale development?

Chapter 5

Attribute #3: Infrastructure

I live in a modest-sized college town. It has a balance of an academic community of university residents and a blue-collar community of healthcare and industry workers. Twenty years ago, you might have considered this a "small town." There was a great little hardware store down the road. It's where everyone went to buy tools, lumber, and lawn and garden materials, pretty much anything you needed to do a project around the house. Fifteen years ago, our first big-box store moved into town, followed quickly by the first large home improvement center. Very soon afterward, our local hardware store closed. Why is that? As our university grew bigger and our industries grew larger, the housing needs of our community increased, and the large big box stores were simply more prepared to grow with this demand than the small hardware store. There was the perception, perhaps accurate, that being able to buy everything you need, and do so in large quantities, was more valuable than even the personalized service the small hardware store might be able to provide. Now in truth, that particular hardware store was geographically challenged in that it was across the street from the first big-box store. Around the town, there still are three or four smaller hardware stores that sell lumber, tools, garden supplies, and all the things we would need, and they employ people who really know their trade. We now have an environment where, based on our needs, we can go to the big-box store or we can go to the smaller stores. If you own a construction company and you're building a dozen homes, you may be more likely to go to the larger store. If you're single homeowner and you're redoing your garden, you have a choice depending on what is most important to you: price, customer service, variety, quantity, quality, etc. I might add that the smaller store is often easier to *get in and get out* compared to the vast size of the larger store, and I can park outside the front door instead of weaving through the vast parking lot; so for a quick one or two item stop, the smaller store is more suitable.

Now imagine that you are a training organization in search of partner to help with training development. Do you need the big-box store, or do you need the small hardware store? Are you developing large volumes for multiple departments, or are you developing a single course for very personally important business objectives? This is where Attribute #3: Infrastructure comes into play. If you are developing an ad-hoc series of training programs, even if you are outsourcing an entire department, but the volume of programs developed simultaneously is a "manageable" quantity (a term that is totally proportional to the size of the provider and open to interpretation), then a smaller provider may very well fit all your needs and be more convenient. You get to park close to the door and get very personal assistance. However, if you are outsourcing an entire division or even your entire company's training development, then you may need a larger provider with more capacity and scalability. In either case, you need to find a provider with a **strong infrastructure.** In the case of the smaller provider, a lack of strong infrastructure is inconvenient. In the case of the larger provider, this attribute is critical and can quickly lead to failure if not solidly fulfilled. Why? If you were acquiring the construction materials for an entire community development project, you would need a large volume of materials, but lumber is lumber, nails are nails, and you're buying products, so the ability to achieve consistent quality from the provider is very predictable. It's unlikely that the length of your nails is going to change radically with each box. However, training development is not like buying the nails. Buying training is more like actually building a house. So acquiring a volume of lumber isn't the hard part; deploying enough high-quality construction workers is your challenge. You would never want to sacrifice the quality of the construction simply because the volume of your housing community is greater. Such is true with training development. It is essential that you have a partner that is able to scale to your needs and **do so without sacrificing quality.**

CENTRALIZED INFRASTRUCTURE

Merely a few years ago, I would've put Process or Technology as Attribute #3, but in recent years, I have learned the critical value of infrastructure and its potential to kill a successful outsourcing relationship. Here's why. Over much of my career, the teams that I worked with were all centrally located together. That included the project teams back in my days with Accenture and E&Y. No matter where the client was, we all went to that client and we worked as a team at the client location. In those days, if the client was out of town, we most likely had an apartment were several of us would stay. Back in 2000, when I led the UNext.com development center, we were again all centrally located. I carried that forward into Option Six. We had one central development center, with only a couple instructional designers working remotely. In a centralized environment, there are things that you take for granted, parts of business that you don't need to worry about in a centralized structure of this nature. For example, any new employee who shows up is instantly surrounded by all the experienced employees. This makes orientation, mentoring, coaching, and accessing answers to that person's questions very seamless. A new person steps into an existing process, with all the support that all the other employees have, and achieves high performance very quickly.

In the absence of a central environment, you have an increased necessity for alternative instruments that can carry through with the needs of a new employee. They are not sitting around the experienced employees or in the mature structure. They may simply be working from home or staffed full-time alone at a client, which makes it more challenging. Without a solid infrastructure, such new employees are on an island, fending for themselves, and very likely not performing at their own potential or the high level that you need. Compound this during a typical new account startup. If one employee is struggling, what happens when you need to hire 20? Even the centralized environment scenario is not immune. While the experienced culture may absorb a single new employee very efficiently, if the orientation process and supporting instruments have not been formalized, then the need to absorb 20 new employees, and do so quickly, will be likewise challenging.

This attribute applies more strongly to the vendor than it does to a typical corporation. Corporations don't often have to worry about scalability at the same magnitude that a provider might. It's unlikely that a corporation would start a new initiative that instantly needs 50 new people to execute it—not impossible, but rare. Whereas, when a vendor wins the new account, especially a large account, they may need to hire many new people in a very short period of time. This includes the reallocation of existing employees to the new account very quickly. You must amass a team that can work very effectively together. So how do you do that? When they find the people, how do they train them and how do they determine the best role for them? When they're on the job, who answers their questions, who checks their work, who ensures that the quality you demand is being produced? These are only some of the dependencies of infrastructure.

THE PLAGUE: JUST-IN-TIME HIRING

The antithesis of a solid infrastructure is the **horror** of *just-in-time hiring*. Let's set the stage. If you're in a corporation, then you are most likely in a situation where you cannot hire a new employee unless you have the position approved—meaning there is a budget for that position. Once approved, you would search and try to find the most experienced person you can, but the person doesn't have to be here tomorrow and you have time to make sure you make the right hire; then you have time for them to get acclimated to the job, perhaps to be around other people doing similar jobs. Obviously, there are exceptions. However, if you are a provider, you do not have the same luxury on either end: time to hire or time to acclimate. You cannot be in a situation where you have to hire someone new every time you get a new account. You cannot wait until you have a position approved before you start to seek someone to hire. When you have won the deal, and the client has selected you to help solve their problems, then they expect you to assign someone immediately. Very likely, the client did not hire you with four months advanced notice. Chances are good that when they hired you, they had an immediate need, and they want you to assign your best people. In a *just-in-time* hiring model, you will fail because you don't have existing employees available. Why would they be sitting around? Typically, the existing employees are busy at another client. Instead, you're forced to find someone new. That means you need to take time to look for them, qualify them, negotiate with them, hire them, and on-board them. This is a very real issue. Some of the most disastrous examples I've seen were a result of just-in-time hiring. The provider wasn't prepared, the timeline to acquire employees was too long, and there were inadequate orientation programs, so the client didn't get the A-team. The client got whoever was available while the provider had to pay whatever that person required because there wasn't enough time to negotiate. It's a terrible circumstance.

Let's look at a different situation that was unsuccessful. This involved a fairly large engagement where the vendor was selected because of its size, its global reach, and the thousands and thousands of employees that it promoted during the proposal process. This vendor won a very large account to produce hundreds of courses every year. It was expected that it would take 40 or more people to do the job, but here's the problem. The vendor didn't have an office in that city, and they didn't have a central development center with capacity; therefore, the vendor had to either transfer or hire all 40 of those people. They relocated two account managers who had experience. That's a great start, but what about the people actually doing the work? This is where infrastructure becomes so important. Can the provider scale quickly to 40 people and still ensure stability and quality? That's where this company struggled. They had very few people to transfer and needed to hire 40 people off the street, but they did not have a robust orientation or support program, so they had to rely on each individual's experience. As I established earlier, we're in an industry without standards, so your reliance on an individual's experience can leave you at *any place on the map*. Within the first year, they had a 50-percent turnover rate on the team; these people were either rejected by the client or simply burned out by the demands. (Remember, what we do is hard, and only the strong survive.) By the second year, they had stabilized the environment, and they continued to produce good results for the client, but the lack of a strong infrastructure was a key to the early failure that almost killed the relationship.

RISKY BUSINESS

This particular attribute is one where you must be very, very cognizant in the proposal process. You must be careful to ensure that the provider's salespeople represent their company without stretching the edges of honesty and stay safely back to the point where nobody gets hurt. I've had a very successful track record of winning proposals; I can spin yarn with the best of them, but I always make sure that the promises I make can adequately be fulfilled by my teams. For example, a provider can tout their methodology and the fact that it's trademarked, even display it with lots of pictures, boxes, and arrows, without noting whether any of their employees actually follow it. The sales representatives might get away with it, but then delegate the responsibility on the operations team, who then must fulfill the promises. (We talked about this in the methodology attribute.)

The infrastructure is a dangerous consideration in the proposal process, and unfortunately, it's perhaps the easiest one for the sales team to fudge. Larger providers can come into a proposal process and tout the thousands of employees who work for them and their global reach into all the different countries. This may be true—they may have thousands of employees, and they may be located all over the globe—but the other thing that is most certainly true is that **every one of them is busy.** If you have a new account and you're going to need 40 people, it does not matter who you select; they most likely do not have 40 of their best people sitting around waiting for your phone call.

So this is where infrastructure is seriously important and why it rates as Attribute #3. **If the vendor does not have the adequate infrastructure, then they cannot scale to meet demand without sacrificing quality.** A strong infrastructure will allow a company, within a reasonable period of time, to adequately scale to meet the client's demand. You can't fake an infrastructure, but you can identify if there is one.

WHAT IS INFRASTRUCTURE?

Infrastructure, simply put, is the vendor's ability to support a scalable business model without sacrificing quality. This gets to the very heart of the business practice. It addresses the many back-office functions—HR, accounting, sales, and so on—that can have an impact on the success of the outsourcing relationship.

First, do they have hiring practices that allow them to identify, validate, and negotiate with high-quality staff **proactively**? In a consulting organization, it is fundamental to keep the recruiting engine humming. Finding talented individuals in the training industry is very difficult. Earlier, we established that there are no standards and the quality of people who call themselves instructional designers varies widely.

Once the provider brings in the new employees, what processes are they following to make sure that those employees can function at the highest level? Are they bringing them into a development center of dozens of other employees who understand the job, or is the new employee working from home? Obviously, the thoroughness and rigidity required of the on-boarding processes varies in the two situations. Do they have ongoing support and development opportunities for the employees? Not the traditional conference attendance or weekend courses, but rather an ability to share lessons learned and successes across the organization. (Some people refer to them as brown-bag sessions.)

THE ART OF OUTSOURCE ACCOUNTING

The requirements of infrastructure are not simply about scaling the number of employees. It also includes other elements of the business operations that may affect the success of the relationship. For example, the provider's financial administration processes can either help facilitate a smooth and seamless relationship or they can hamper the process by making it frustrating to do business with them. Let me give you an example: In the custom development of training, we typically go through several phases. This is not unique; we start with the design phase, then the development phase, testing phase, and installation phase. Each of these phases may include one or more deliverables: the documents and/or versions of the course that are approved at various stages of the project. These deliverables are outlined in the sales process, the proposal, and the statement of work. Typically, the projected date of completion is indicated with a price for each deliverable. That's a pretty common situation. As each deliverable is approved, the provider submits an invoice, the client approves the invoice, and the provider gets paid. Simple as that! Right?

For vendors on a cash-based system, this works out just fine. Send an invoice, get paid, deposit cash, and credit the books. For companies on an accrual-based system, this process gets trickier, and if not aligned well, it can cause major issues within the relationship. In the accrual process, the arrival of the cash is relatively irrelevant; the accountants will recognize the revenue either when the actual deliverable is complete and the invoice is submitted, or they will accrue the revenue based on the timeline and labor. Okay, that starts to sound complicated, and it can be if not aligned effectively. Misalign these processes, and way too many conversations and wasted time is spent determining what has been "recognized" and balancing the monthly accounts.

For example, one provider was practicing in the training development arena, but their origin was as a product-based business. They were used to billing the client when the product was delivered. Now the issue they faced was mapping their financial structure to training development projects. Based on the standard corporate accounting process, they would recognize revenue once the project was complete, but here's the problem. Unlike delivering an already complete product from inventory, you have to actually develop the training product and finance the development along the way. That means the project, which may take anywhere from six weeks to six months, and earn tens of thousands or hundreds of thousands of dollars, does not recognize a single cent until the project is finished. The provider's development team (division, department, group, however they are organized) absorbs all the labor costs before recognizing the revenue, *from an accounting standpoint*. In reality, the deliverables are still invoiced and paid, but the accountants don't recognize them because they don't fit their model.

Why should you care? Because the people on that project would rather not wait until the end of the project to get paid. The development operations are incurring costs throughout the entire project without being awarded the revenue. Again, why should you care? Because when issues of this nature are not aligned with the way the business will be conducted, it becomes a tremendous distraction to the account managers and project managers. Instead of focusing on the development of your courseware, they are focused on managing their finances (and arguing with their accounting group about why this or that should have been recognized). In nearly all provider organizations, the account managers and project managers are assessed upon their profitability. If they are incurring costs, but not recognizing the revenue, then their numbers look bad, and lots of time is wasted updating spreadsheets.

Another area to consider is the salesperson's compensation. Are they compensated in a manner that benefits the relationship? For example, if they received a commission for the initial sale, was it based on what you *thought* you might order or for what you actually did order? Are they compensated for the future work, and are they compensated for the future work regardless of whether they were involved in it? These are not questions that are typically considered in the vendor relationship, but I have found that these questions are incredibly important to ensure that the infrastructure is in place and that these issues will not be a distraction, but rather *strengthen* the relationship. Behavior follows recognition and compensation. You need to ensure that the sales team has the proper motivations and that they align with your needs. I have witnessed situations where the salesperson receives a commission on the *initial* sale but will not receive commissions on follow-up work unless they're involved. What happens in that situation is that the salesperson becomes a gatekeeper. And why wouldn't they? I would not want someone else talking to my client if it meant I would not get paid for it. Likewise, I have seen the situation with a salesperson makes the sale, gets the commission, and then leaves. Never to be seen again, and occasionally calling in for more work. This doesn't help the team and typically annoys the client.

THE BUYER'S INFRASTRUCTURE

I recognize that much of this applies to the provider side, for all the obvious reasons, but there are clear infrastructure factors on the corporate side. They may include business administration, getting budgets approved, getting invoices approved, getting vendors online, getting vendors paid—all come to play and can influence the success of the training organization and/or the success of an outsourcing operation. I recall one example where a provider won the sole source contract with a large pharmaceutical company. The relationship started immediately with frustration as the processes put in place for requesting new projects, completing and signing SOWs, and using subcontractors were so laborious that business initiatives started to stall and the company's training groups started working around the sole source agreement just to get their work completed on time.

Did I mention getting the vendor paid? Some of the more successful relationships I had during the early days of Option Six were with the client who had flexible payment schedules. At times, I might have to give up a percent or two in exchange for a faster payment, but the smaller firms benefit from that. Some of the worst relationships I've seen are with clients, or small providers who are subcontracting to larger providers, who have rigid payment schedules, typically very long (I had a recent gig where the payment term was 79 days!), and the larger providers didn't mind delaying at the end of any quarter. Long delays in payment to any provider will adversely affect the business. A larger company will suffer from the distractions of chasing down invoices and accounts receivable to meet their monthly goals, while a smaller company may go out of business altogether if they can't pay their employees. As I mentioned earlier, it is very important that the clients keep their vendors in business.

NOT SO OBVIOUS

I want to note that the Infrastructure Attribute includes elements that are certainly not obvious. It takes some digging to recognize the impact and address it early in the relationship. For example, how does the vendor treat its subcontractors, especially if you're going to be working with subject matter that requires third-party expertise or large variable volumes where the vendor may outsource certain courses or parts of the project? The payment terms and administrative processes can have a monstrous impact on the efficiency of an outsourcing arrangement. For example, I once witnessed a project that nearly ended in disaster due to the provider's inability to pay the third-party SME. The project took 16 weeks to complete, and the key team member was a subject matter expert with a very unique understanding of the subject domain. It took 12 weeks before this SME saw his first paycheck. It was only after he threatened to leave the project, thus leaving it in jeopardy, that he got paid. The administrative processes that the subcontractor had to go through in order to receive his payment were not friendly and bordered on absurd.

Another infrastructure area might be the invoicing process and how statements of work are structured. Are they structured in a way that it is friendly to the vendor, meaning they are able to recognize the revenue on a consistent basis, or is the statement of work so detailed that it slows down the project request process or (on the contrary) is too simplified as it doesn't satisfy the requirements of the vendor's own accounting organization. These are non-obvious but very critical considerations informing the outsourcing relationship to ensure that both parties can work effectively.

SCABILITY WITHOUT SACRIFICING QUALITY

The Infrastructure Attribute has many components, but I'll focus on one most notable to illustrate its definition: scalability. There is a recognition that the more effective vendors are also those that can scale quickly to meet your needs. For the very large companies that are outsourcing an entire division and/or very large volumes of training, this is an essential requirement. The question is: Does the vendor have the infrastructure necessary to rapidly scale without sacrificing quality? That latter part is the most essential element. There are lots of large consulting and staffing companies who can very quickly find 20 or 40 people to hire and assign to a client, but in training development, that does not guarantee an effective result.

So when I define infrastructure in terms of scalability, there are two fundamentals: the vendor's ability to leverage existing, experienced employees, and their ability to bring on new employees and make them effective. For existing employees, I suggest reviewing things such as their current available bench strength (keeping in mind that most consulting firms cannot afford to simply keep people idle in anticipation of future projects) and their current utilization rate. Is their run rate so high that they are very thin and unlikely to have lots of bandwidth from existing employees to work on your account? Is utilization at a manageable rate where there is a possibility that existing experienced employees will be available to lead and assist in the coaching of new employees brought on as a result of this increased volume of work? For new employees, I'd want to know about their on-boarding process—not simply the standard compliance course that we're all forced to take, but rather courses that help build a full understanding of the methodology, processes, tools, standards, and expectations. This is the key differentiator. During the research process, I was startled to discover that a very large number of providers do **not** have a formal on-boarding process; in other words, they do not have a series of training programs that all new employees do in order to understand how to do their work.

Another vital aspect of infrastructure deals with the recruiting process. Has the vendor created a "stable" of qualified talent, available for them to engage quickly for your needs? Have they spent the time to identify and find these candidates, pretest their skills if necessary, and negotiate an effective rate? I've seen organizations running so thin and with human resource practices that are so strict, they ended up in a *just-in-time* recruiting process. That is a fundamental point of failure in training development outsourcing. The work required in training development is difficult and challenging. You're paying big money to hire a provider to do the work for you. Do you want a provider who pulls the first warm body off the street and assigns them to your projects? In short, most every project that we address has a very fixed timeline, the vendor selection process always takes longer than expected, and the client wants to start right away. Any vendor whose infrastructure forces them to wait until the project has a full "green light" before even seeking the right staff is ultimately going to end up with someone who is simply "available" and costs more than necessary. You want a provider with a strong recruiting practice, a healthy stable of qualified candidates, and maybe even a strong freelance contracting practice that provides variable labor to support your needs.

BUILDING THE CULTURE

When I started my career at Andersen Consulting, now called Accenture, I spent a good part of my time in the small town of St. Charles, Illinois. Andersen was a company that was growing exceptionally fast and needed a very effective way of bringing in new talent—to orient them to the Andersen culture, and teach them the skills and behaviors necessary to be successful at the client. It was an amazing experience, one that I know was expensive for the firm, and a program that certainly gave them a competitive edge over everyone else. This was a unique opportunity for the new staff to gain instruction by experienced staff (all the instructors were experienced consultants and not simply full-time facilitators) and to interact with each other. The new employees were from all regions and countries where Andersen served. It was a long six-week process, including three weeks of self-study in our home office and three weeks at St. Charles. By the time we left the training program, we were all *speaking the same language* (of business anyway), using the same terminology, employing a uniform skill set, and fully understanding what the firm expected from us. That was the first benefit of the St. Charles environment.

There was a second benefit of the St. Charles environment. This was also where nearly all the training for the company's internal usage was developed. The staff and experts required for a training program were all centrally located in St. Charles for the duration of the project. This ensured that all the talent necessary was quickly accessible, working together, and achieved a high level of efficiency, allowing us to produce products faster and with a higher degree of quality.

Now you may read this and think "Good for them. They're the largest consulting company on the planet." That is true, but the fundamentals don't change. If you want to be successful, you must have a way to ensure that all your employees have a uniform capability, understand what you demand from them, and are prepared to provide high-quality service. You may not need your own campus, but you do need your own program. I've seen this model work in consulting companies of all sizes, and I've seen them become highly successful, highly efficient, and produce outstanding quality.

I'm biased toward centralized development and the implementation of development centers. The boutique companies that do training development and are all located under one roof have been more successful, from what I have seen, than those who are merely a network of freelancers all working from home. I have seen this model mapped to some of the largest providers in the training industry, where their talent pool is located in multiple development centers across the country, perhaps across the world. Unfortunately, I have also been exposed to large development companies that continue to use a decentralized organizational alignment, where everyone works from home and all the functional resources necessary—media, writing, programming, design—are distributed. My bias stems from the high degree of consistent success I've witnessed by centralized companies and the high degree of failures that I've witnessed from the organizations who attempt to support development with a decentralized organization structure.

As I stated earlier, when all your resources are under one roof, you have many options when it comes to scalability. The ability to conduct orientation sessions using experienced staff as the instructors and pulling the new staff together to share the experience is much simpler because everyone is in one spot. It is expensive to do this in a decentralized environment due to the need to fly everyone in—often cost-prohibitive. Very few companies have the budgets to fly all employees to a concentrated orientation session, so they either attempt to conduct it virtually or, more often, neglect it altogether.

A central environment also enables strong mentorship, the ability to partner inexperienced staff with experienced staff, working side-by-side, together on projects, doing the same type of work. The *speed to performance* in that environment is much faster. The objective of achieving a uniform quality and level of efficiency is much more possible. In a decentralized structure, every individual is on his or her own to achieve the level of performance required. Mentorships may be possible, but again it's decentralized or not working side-by-side, and does not get the same support.

Why is this important? Let me give you an example. One of my highest achievements was winning a very large account with a massive financial services company. To fulfill their needs, we needed to add 20 people to our staff within six weeks. Imagine the process of identifying those 20 people, negotiating their salaries, hiring them, bringing them on, orienting them to our way of doing business, orienting them to the client's needs, introducing them to our methodology and processes, teaching them how to use our tools, and determining whether they were a good cultural fit and had the full potential to deliver on our promise. Whew. It was all very daunting; it was lots of work and extremely important and fragile because we had a new client who was depending on us to do so effectively. Hiring these 20 people off the street and attempting to achieve uniform capability would be impossible.

We benefited from the fact that we already had centralized development centers. We dedicated one of the development centers to providing this service; that development center was already serving a handful of large clients and was doing so very effectively. Focusing this development center on the new client and building the new staff in an environment filled with highly successful individuals enabled us to achieve our objective. Existing employees within that development center were assigned while new employees were added to the team. It was still lots of work, but we were doing it with seasoned employees all under one roof.

THE FINAL QUESTION

To summarize, here are the key questions that you are trying to answer in this attribute:

- Do they need a sustainable staffing model? Can they scale quickly without sacrificing quality?

- Do they maintain a healthy utilization level and maintain a (reasonable) bench of available staff? Do they have the staff that you need now?

- Do they have a proactive recruiting process that provides a stable of available candidates? Or do they use just-in-time staffing once the projects are sold?

- What are the qualifications and experience (as an employee of the vendor) for each level of management assigned to the account?

- Do their financial processes align with yours? Are there ways to structure the SOW and invoicing processes to benefit both parties?

- Does their sales commission structure support long-term involvement with the relationship, or just the initial sales gains?

Seven Attributes Framework

Chapter 6

Attribute #4: Process

What do an architect and an instructional designer have in common? Not as much as they should. With an architect, they work closely with the client to determine the client's needs. They then draft a series of blueprints, periodically reviewing those with the client to make sure that the needs are being met, get their input, and brainstorm ideas for the final design; then once the blueprints are approved, the architect begins working with the construction crew and the general contractor, and the subcontractors begin to get involved in the project. There is a constant collaboration between the architect, the client, and the general contractor. As the house begins to take shape, often things that were unforeseen need to be discussed and decided, such as the angle of a wall, the height of a doorway, the configuration of a closet, the selection of certain interior lighting, etc. This is the collaborative, team-based environment of an architect.

What you will not see is the architect with a hammer in his hand banging away at wood and raising walls. You don't see the architect lay down the wires, fix the plumbing, hang the light fixtures, or paint the walls. No, instead it is a collaborative process among a team of specialists (carpenters, plumbers, painters, etc.), and each one has a unique talent and role on the project. Through a refined and collaborative process, the house begins to take shape, and with constant involvement of the client and the architect, and a really solid construction team, you general end up with a very beautiful result. This is an *uncommon* process within training development.

Imagine if you could apply that process to training development. Imagine if you had an instructional designer, much like the architect, who you could work with side-by-side to ensure that you're always on track and make the decisions and minor adjustments needed during the process. Isn't that the partner you would prefer?

In this world, you would also want the confidence that the structural integrity of your product was just as good as every other product produced by this contractor. That would be true if you were building a house, and it should be true if you're building a training program. What if you could ensure that every element of your training program was built by an expert in that element? Much like the plumber focuses on the water flow and the electrician focuses on the power, you would have specialists focused on the graphics and the media, the technical aspects, the writing of the content, the overall design of the learning experience, perhaps even the user experience/usability of the training. I would suggest that the success rate of this provider is a single instructional designer *swinging his or her* own hammer.

We have a phrase that we use in our practice: the least common denominator. When applied to training development, this describes a situation where you are building a product that requires multiple elements of that product to be at their most effective state, elements where certain professionals have an expertise in the development of this, such as a graphic artist developing media objects or someone with an English or journalism background writing the content to the reading level of the audience, but you are in a situation where a <u>single</u> individual, who may have experience developing each of the elements, but who is not an expert in <u>all</u> the elements. The resulting product reflects the least common denominator. It is the best that the individual is capable of producing within each function.

Now contrast that with a scenario where you have formed a team of individuals, all working together, applying their expertise to each element, and thus achieving the highest quality possible for each element. Let's face it; not all instructional designers are great writers. Not all great writers understand the art and science of adult learning. Few instructional designers would classify themselves as artists, thus having to resort to clipart or draft their media ideas on paper and send it to a programmer, perhaps in a different country, to produce the final results.

THE CREATIVE PROCESS

So what's the real driving force behind the process? Inherently, the big issue with the development of any learning solution is that it is "squishy." You're not dealing with a tangible raw material. We're not making tires or silicon chips. No, we're not building houses. While a solid instructional designer will develop a detailed design plan for the program, it is not until you get into the detail of the content that you really understand what it is you're trying to build and the best way to build it. We are dealing with knowledge. We are dealing with the ideas and information in the heads of our subject matter experts. At times, these could be concrete and extremely well-documented in standard operating procedures or a user's manual, but that is a very rare situation. What we typically get instead is an idea, a vision. We probably have a client with a business problem they are trying to solve. They may be introducing a new product to their customers, changing their marketing strategy, increasing the financial capabilities of their staff, upgrading the leadership's skills, installing a new information system, etc. The client has a vision, a need, and a goal to achieve. The challenge for us emerges when the raw material for meeting this goal is "squishy." It is not firmly documented, nor could it be. If it is a new product, a new initiative, a new system, then often these items are under development while we are trying to develop the learning solution. This is a common situation. Any instructional

109

designer who believes that a subject matter expert can hand them a stack of content and they in turn can mold that into an effective learning experience by themselves has not been in the industry very long.

I had a pharmaceutical company as a client. They had a very respected brand and high-demand products, but they screwed up. Someone made a mistake. Someone sent an email to all the users of their product, but used the CC field on the message instead of the BCC field. Thus, everyone on the list saw names of every other user. Obviously, the federal government wasn't impressed. The company was levied with fines and told that everyone in the company must complete consumer privacy training. Thus, they needed a course. They are multi-national, so they wanted an online course for rapid distribution. The vendor they hired held several meetings with the client, gathered all the source materials, and then disappeared for two months. When they returned with their storyboards, the course wasn't anything near what the client expected. They provided lots of feedback, and the vendor went off again for another four weeks. When they returned, the course still was not what the clients wanted, and now the deadline loomed over them. They were forced to find another firm, in this case mine, to salvage the project. This is an example of the linear process to the extreme. It simply doesn't work in the development of training programs that address intangible subjects. The client needs to be able to see the product, early and often.

You cannot approach the development of a learning solution as a linear process, like we would the building of a house or silicon chips. It is a creative process. You are molding a product out of an intangible raw material. Imagine that you are a sculptor and not an assembly line worker. The issue with most training development companies is that they attempt to approach each project as an assembly line. They believe that with a couple of sessions with a subject matter expert, a couple of interviews, the review of source materials, and enough time to themselves, they can craft the perfect solution. Further, when developing training programs for online delivery, web-based or mobile, that they can construct the learning experience on paper, do a review with the subject matter expert on paper, send it off to some programmers to put it online, conduct another review with a subject matter expert, and call it done. It's not that simple. It's a creative process that requires lots of iterative development between the designers and the subject matter experts. It requires the ability to view the product *early and often* throughout the process to ensure that the intangible raw materials are being translated and converted into an **accurate and effective** learning program. This requires a process that enables the iterative development, that enables the frequent review, and that continuously hones the knowledge of the subject matter experts into a solution that will meet the learner's needs.

AVOID THE ASSEMBLY LINE

I was exposed to a large training development outsource provider who attempted to approach training development as an assembly line process. They actually outlined in their statement of work with the client that there would be no fewer than 10 percent changes at the Alpha. Let me reflect. They believed that if they held an all-day session with the subject matter experts and gathered all the source materials available to them, they could produce a version of the training program that was 90 percent complete upon its first review. That was bold. The big issue for the training development company in this scenario is not simply the obvious fact that they cannot achieve a 90 percent accuracy rate on the very first review, but believing that they can lead the team to burn a proportional amount of the overall project budget getting to this first review, then facing the fact that they've achieved less than 90 percent, and thus have an unexpected amount of additional work waiting for them to be performed with the remaining budget. Not surprising, with this client, their largest problem within the organization was profitability. You may recall from the beginning of this book when I defined "success" as the equilibrium where the client's vision is achieved and the vendor makes a profit? I've just outlined a scenario where the client's vision is clearly not being achieved and the vendor is clearly not going to make a profit.

This isn't the only example I've seen. In fact, an exceptionally large percentage of the providers in our industry continue to approach training development as if it were an assembly line process, instead of the creative iterative process that it truly is. With the successful providers I've seen, they approached the process as an *active refinement*. We often refer to it as "get it wrong as fast as we can, so we can start working on getting it right." I once got into a near shouting match with an account manager who insisted "we can't possibly allow our clients to make changes after Alpha." That account manager, in a multimillion dollar engagement, struggled to make a profit consistently. The reason? By believing that training development can be produced in a linear pattern, that they would get it right the first time, and that they could muscle their SMEs to limit their changes. If you acknowledge that the process is not linear, that you are more likely to get it wrong the first time, that the SMEs will react, digest, reconsider, and respond with unexpected results, and therefore that you will need more effort after the reviews than before, you must design a process that can be flexible and be successful in that environment.

As W. Edwards Deming has said, **"If you take really good people and put them in a bad process, the process will win**

every time." This is exceptionally true in the area of training development. The structure of the workflow, the composition of the team, your ability to be flexible, and the efficiency of the overall project are all determinants of a good process or a bad process. The process includes things such as the workflow and how tasks are assigned, the way you interact with your subject matter experts, the content draft and review process, the user testing process (if any), the technical integration process, the way a global team might be used, project management, document management, status reviews, and the overall governing process. These are all elements of the process that determines the outcome of a project. If your vendor does not have a strong process, then the talent level of their employees won't matter. They will not be able to achieve the potential and not achieve your vision.

THE USAGE OF TEAMS

The highly effective development providers I have seen are those that apply a team process, a collaborative approach working tightly with the subject matter experts, the client, and the stakeholders, and deploying a team of experts, working together to form an exceptional result. The providers that I have seen struggle are those with the *"one size fits all"* instructional designer who does all the work from the very beginning to the very end, with the probable exception of the media within an online course. This is very similar to the architect swinging a hammer. Sure, maybe some architects are good with a hammer, but it is not always a good use of their time or talent; they are taking on tasks for which they are not strongest and neglecting the tasks that most need their expertise.

The teams that I have seen that have been highly effective are those that follow a collaborative process.

The project team would include an instructional designer who would be the key individual in the relationship with the client and the subject matter experts. The ID would be the one who creates the design documents and works in collaboration with the client to refine these documents through a couple iterations. Then, the ID would assign specialists to specific tasks within development—the tasks where a specialist is much more likely to produce effective results. For example, often a content developer, writer, or editor would be used to work in collaboration with the instructional designer throughout development, much like the architect works with the general contractor. Now, why would you use a content developer instead of allowing the instructional designer to complete the development? The answer is quite simple. A good content developer has an educational background and experience in the art of writing. The instructional designer, a good one, has a strong educational background and experience in the area of instructional design—the way people learn. They are not the same thing. Determining the best way to structure the content to be effective versus actually aggregating all the content into a common voice accessible to the target audience takes a different skill set.

The other key team member is the media developer. In a classroom setting, or possibly through virtual instructional, a media developer affects the overall learning experience. The media developer is focused on visuals and graphics. For online learning program, the media developer is focused on the graphics, but also the animations and any interactive objects within the course. The highly effective training organizations that I have witnessed are those where the media developer is an integrated member of the project team from the very beginning. This person attends design sessions, attends status report meetings, and works with the training developer and the instructional designer on media scripts develop and media ideas are envisioned.

If you involve the media developer early and often, he or she grows an understanding of the overall course, of the subject matters expert's interests, of the learner's needs—an understanding that is perhaps not quite as deep as an instructional designer, but thorough enough that the instructional designer does not have to be prescriptive or minutely detailed in their written communication to the developer. This is an indication of a highly efficient process. Because the media developer has this understanding and has been part of the project, the instructional designer does not need detailed storyboards. Certainly, some storyboards are useful for outlining complex animations or simulations, but these are now the exception to the rule. If the media developer has a solid understanding of the course and has gained a good understanding of the subject matter, he or she is exceptionally helpful at envisioning media ideas and then developing the media objects without a detailed storyboard. What I have witnessed most with this alignment is that instructional designers and subject matter experts come up with really good ideas for media, and then they meet with the media developer and find out that the media developer can realize those ideas and add to them. The media developer's understanding and expertise in media, and what the tools can provide, will often produce results even better than the instructional designer had envisioned.

Now, on the contrary, the result is quite different and less efficient for the project teams that do not include a media developer throughout the project. These are often providers who are outsourcing media development to another company or another country. The requirement in this circumstance is a very detailed and rigid storyboard by the instructional designer that will enable a media developer, who has been working in a vacuum, to understand their full intention and produce a result that matches the instructional designer's vision. This is daunting. We have all seen the circumstances: The media developer never gets it right the first time. How could he? It's the first time he has seen or even heard of the course and/or subject matter. A process that treats the training development as an assembly line, with the hope that one individual (the instructional designer or "architect") can do all the work or dictate all the work is not an efficient process. This issue of working as an assembly line, detailing every aspect of the course on a storyboard, sending those storyboards to the other side of the planet, and expecting a perfect result is simply not realistic.

SMEs and ITERATIVE DEVELOPMENT

The key to an effective project experience is a solid relationship between the development team and the subject matter experts. Perhaps the biggest challenge of all is that everyone is busy. The subject matter experts assigned to you are probably the boldest and brightest employees in that domain. They are probably not sitting around waiting for you to call them to ask for information. They are probably the employees in highest demand, so they have very little time to spare. If your interaction with the subject matter expert is going to be truly effective, the SME needs to feel that the time is well spent. If they feel that your interaction with them is concise, to the point, productive, and they "only have to say it once," then they will respond to your emails and answer your phone calls. If they feel that their time is wasted or your response has not been thorough, then they are less likely to respond.

Unfortunately, given that the SMEs are busy, they may not always be able to respond as fast as you would like. You may request two days from them to review a piece of content. That two-day window may even be defined in the vendor's contract with the client, but if the subject matter expert is not available for those two days, then it doesn't matter. What's my point? Your process must be **flexible.** The vendor must be able to accelerate or decelerate the timeline to accommodate the availability of your client. They must also be able to find creative ways to stay productive and moving forward in the event that the SME is not available as often as you wish. This piece is challenging no doubt. It may very well require that some of the project team become pseudo-experts in the subject themselves or find other means of gathering the information outside the prime subject matter expert. *This is what separates the men from the boys.* If the team gets frustrated because the subject matter expert is unavailable, they can elevate that to a project manager or to the account manager, who will then have frustrating conversations with the key client or stakeholder, but that's not likely to get you any response. Unless it's a situation when the subject matter expert is simply belligerent, there is very little that they can do, so deal with it! With a highly effective process and the right talent on your team this very common occurrence does not need to be a detriment to the project.

Therefore, the next major component of a process that you must assess in your provider deals with the content drafting and subject matter expert review process. As we all know, this is the most important part of a project. Without content, we don't have training. The instructional designer is at a disadvantage. Typically, they are not experts in the subject; that is the role of the subject matter expert, who is often the highest performing individual in the organization. This means that the subject matter expert is also very busy, yet the instructional designer needs their time.

How your training organization and your vendor work through this issue is of paramount importance to the success of the projects. Without an effective process, the instructional designer doesn't get what they need from the subject matter expert, and the subject matter expert doesn't enjoy the process. This leads to many delays and often inadequate results. With a highly effective content development and SME review process, work gets done on time, the subject matter expert may actually enjoy the process, and the instructional designer is able to stay focused because they have the information they need. How do you do this? There are lots of ways and, as I stated earlier; how your vendor approaches this delicate question must be a key factor in your outsourcing decision.

One of the more successful processes I have seen to address this challenge is what I might call an "iterative trickle." The standard process is for the instructional designer to draft all the content into a series of storyboards, usually looking like a series of PowerPoint slides, and then at key points in the project, give the stack of storyboards to the subject matter expert with a firm deadline of x-number of days to review all the storyboards, indicate all the changes, and send the results back to the instructional designer. We already discussed how rarely this turns out as planned. In any highly effective process, the content exchange between the instructional designer and the subject matter expert is in small chunks, the iterative trickle. The instructional designer sends a chunk of content to the subject matter expert, who then reads, edits, revises, comments, and returns it. The chunks are often in 300 words or less (an entirely arbitrary number), a manageable amount of content that enables the SME to read and respond, and then return their focus to their job.

ONLINE PROCESS FOR AN ONLINE PRODUCT

The electrician does not wait until the house is completed before turning on the switch to see if the lights work. The plumber does not wait until the house is completed before turning on the water to see if the faucets work. What we do in training development is very complex. The subject matter that we deal with is often complicated, ambiguous, constantly being redefined, and hard to nail down. Explaining this information to learners and giving them exercises to practice to demonstrate that they have understood the information and can practice it in the real world is a challenge. If you are developing a classroom course and you get this wrong, then perhaps you have an experienced instructor who can fill in the gaps, drag a couple war stories out of their vault, remediate, and help the students along. However, if you are building an online course, you do not have an instructor to do these things. Therefore, you must ensure the course is *rock solid* before the learners take it. The only way to achieve this is with real user testing. The most effective training development providers I have seen are the ones who can facilitate the user test multiple times during the development process.

You might use various names to refer to these points in time. Many organizations refer to them as the Alpha or Beta review with the subsequent final or Gold or Gamma review. Regardless of what they are called, these are the formal reviews of the entire product, per se. Now, the most common process I have seen, one that I don't endorse, is the one whose goal for the review is merely a paper-based representation of the training that will be reviewed by the subject matter expert. Too often, this may be the first time the subject matter expert has ever seen the course content. The Alpha review may have been conducted as a group session for a half day or longer, or it might have been sent to the subject matter expert with an expectation of a certain number of days to return. The goal of this traditional process would then be to make the changes post-Alpha and then build the online version of the course with the goal of the subject matter expert to review the online course during the Beta process, return their feedback, and allow the team to push forward to completion.

There are two massive problems with this traditional process. First, and this is especially true with online courses, until the subject matter experts and the client are able to see an online version of the course, the feedback that they will give you will be limited only to the accuracy of the content. The ability to assess the learning experience of an online course is nearly impossible on paper. It is not possible to get a true understanding of the learner's experience in the online course without seeing it online. The notion of *an online process for online product* to me seems fairly trivial.

If you are able to provide the SMEs with an online review, then you may be able to produce the "ah ha" moment that you need. One of the more fascinating effects I have witnessed when developing an online course is how the subject matter experts, and often the former instructors, if it is a conversion of the classroom course, react when they first see the online version. It is very much an "ah ha" moment. *They get it.* They understand what the online interpretation will look like. (Now, if the online interpretation of your classroom course is simply a linear presentation of slides and text that mimic the classroom course, then read this section twice!) If it is a true *online learning experience,* which is engaging and uses an instructional design approach that works exceptionally well in an online environment, not a linear presentation of content, then the subject matter expert will begin to think of new ways to structure the content and new activities that could be used. They will, in essence, start *rethinking* the course. The sooner they do that, the better. "Get it wrong as fast as you possibly can, so that you can start getting it right."

The second massive issue when you do not conduct an online review is the impact on the learner experience itself. Until you conduct an online review the **actual target audience,** you cannot honestly answer these questions: Is the course effective? Will it produce the new level of skills necessary to achieve the business objectives? These are the important questions that started your project in the first place; your company had a business objective, determined that a training intervention was the best solution, and then assigned you to build a solution. For the solution to be effective, you must acknowledge that there is a very big difference between an effective learning experience and a presentation of content. If you rely solely on the subject matter expert's input, you will most certainly end up with a very accurate presentation of content, but is it an effective learning experience? You don't know the answer to that question until you show the course to the target learners.

Let us agree that the worst possible time to find out that the learners don't like the course, or are not able to achieve the level of performance necessary to achieve the business objective, is after the training is released. Most certainly that will not make your business sponsors, your subject matter expert, and your learners, anybody who is affected by the skills of these individuals, very happy. The only way to ensure that the learning experience is successful is to show it to the learners, and to do so as soon as possible.

REAL USERS. REAL TESTING.

The highly effective development providers I have witnessed are those who use actual employees, the target learners, as part of the Alpha and Beta review process. It does not take many employees; often we may have three or four, but sometimes more than 10, depending on the course and the interest of the company. It is seldom that we have a client refuse to allow employees to view the course during Alpha and Beta, unless they question the quality of the product at that time. Clearly, if the best you have is a paper-based storyboard, many employees will not be very interested in participating. The providers who are highly effective are those who have very solid materials online at the Alpha and Beta stage; it doesn't have to be "complete" because it's impossible to have all the content you need by Alpha—that would be too much to expect. For an online course, we usually targeted about 70 percent of the course would be complete at Alpha, but it would be a full learning experience. This means all the content that we had to date had been written and put online in a menu that would be used by the final product. It would also have a significant amount of media by the Alpha. Now, not all the media would be completed; oftentimes, the audio on the animations would be from company employees instead of the final talent. If there were holes in the content, then in very large red letters, there would be a placeholder that indicates what is missing. If a media object was missing, we would have a link to a transcript of the media object or perhaps see a storyboard of the animation.

What you're trying to determine at Alpha is whether the structure of the course, the contents and the way we have designed the course, are going to be effective for this audience. What we would then hope to achieve is to receive feedback from these reviewers, make the appropriate changes, fill in the holes with the missing content and media objects, and then produce a Beta version. Again, we would have multiple employees from the target audience taking the Beta, adding their content comments, and determining whether it was an effective learning experience. Often, for Beta, we would target a 90 percent completion of the materials. Again, not 100 percent because it's not 100 percent, until everything is finalized, but we did expect that there were no glaring holes and we felt pretty confident about the condition of the course.

One of my favorite examples of a solid Alpha was a course we produced on clinical trials for a large pharmaceutical company. We released the Alpha to a small number of employees, who to our surprise then forwarded it to nearly all the employees in the labs. Even though the course was not complete, it was the first time they'd seen the full clinical trials process clearly described. We still had work to complete, but already the course was providing value. Needless to say, the feedback we received from the Alpha was very robust.

Now, what does it take to achieve this? First, if you're building an online course, your provider must have an online development process in order to achieve an online product by Alpha. In the highly effective organizations I have witnessed, the content developer (that I mentioned earlier in this section) is creating the course online in the course environment, not simply on paper.

This is inherently challenging if your only means of putting a course online is send it to programmers—often individuals who are not in your location and often not in your country—and wait for the results. That turnaround time tends to be a huge stigma in the process.

Second, your provider must have a very effective process for content drafting and subject matter expert review. As I outlined in the earlier examples with the *iterative trickle* review process, if you are sharing content with the subject matter expert in small chunks, they are continuously responding, and you're getting comments and corrections, then the subject matter expert should have seen the entire contents of the course prior to the test, albeit not aggregated. Thus, they can focus on whether the course is an effective learning experience. Let me repeat that point. By the time the SME reviews the Alpha or Beta, they have already reviewed all the content. The last thing you would want in your Alpha or Beta test is a subject matter expert who spends all his time correcting the content because either the changes weren't included or the initial drafting review process wasn't effective. That would be disastrous. Instead, you want the subject matter expert to be able to experience the course the way a learner would experience it.

To adopt this process, you must set the expectation for every employee. When I owned Option Six, I would often conduct one phase of the new employee orientation sessions. One of the lessons I tried to instill in the staff is that they **must be ready for change.** If they approach these projects as a rigid assembly and assume that they will get it right the first time, then they will be very frustrated with the process. If they understand that it is a creative process, a collaborative process, and the purpose of their *first* attempt will be to trigger the response that will lead to the *best* attempt, then they will succeed. Flexibility in this area is immensely important.

PILOT TESTS HAPPEN TOO LATE

Now, those previous scenarios reflected online training. I spend lots of time focusing on online training because a growing amount of our industry's solutions are online products, and they tend to be the most challenging to create. In a classroom training program, the primary instruments are paper or PowerPoint slides—technologies that are very rudimentary for most instructional design teams. For classroom training, the learner experience can only be achieved by having a classroom with people attending the course. That often requires a pilot test. That is an experience where we must bring in more employees and have real instructors. It is a daunting process because often you must create all the materials, but it is fundamental to determine the effectiveness.

The inherent problem with most pilot tests is the instructional teams wait till the very end of the project to conduct them. They assume that they "have it right." My presumption is that if you wait until the end of the project to have your pilot test then, you're simply looking for *validation* that everything you did at that point was correct. What happens if the pilot test fails? We've all seen them fail. What if the participants find it an ineffective instructional experience? What if we discover that we are wrong, that perhaps a module or two fell flat, was confusing, or was unnecessary, or there was another major deviation? If you wait until the end, then you have not left yourself much time after the pilot to make the required changes.

I once was party to a project for a global technology company that was revamping part of their marketing strategy. The modality selected was a blended solution. It included an online course, followed by a classroom course. The stakeholder and SME conducted all the content and course reviews. The online course was effectively user tested during the Alpha and Beta phases using actual employees from the target audience. However, the pilot test for the classroom session was held at the end of the project. The session was held in Orlando during this company's global staff conference. The attendees were not only the target audience, but also key decision makers in the marketing group. To say that the pilot test was a disaster would be an understatement. I felt sorry for the instructors who were constantly peppered with questions, contradictions, and noted inaccuracies. (It was also unfair that most of the participants didn't complete the online course.) In several parts of the course, the content was "technically" accurate, in this case the new market strategy, but it did not effectively reflect the way the content would be implemented in their practice. The issue was that the course was never really user tested to validate the context. The pilot test was, of course, the last step of the project and not nearly enough time had been reserved to make adjustments, especially not of this magnitude. Suffering from failure of the pilot left a terrible impression on the vendor and delayed the launch of the market strategy, and the client-side project manager left for another employer.

Remember, it is much better to *get it wrong faster* and leave yourself time to get it right. A pilot test earlier in the process, even if it is incomplete, even if you were not sure of its quality, would be much more effective to your efforts at achieving a successful results compared to a pilot test at the end. If the pilot test at the end falls flat, then you'll most certainly end up with uncomfortable conversations with your client about missing your deadlines because you have not left yourself enough time to make the changes that are necessary.

AGILE

One of the more successful development outsourcing companies I've seen took the standard methodology of ADDIE and integrated it with the standard methodology for software development (SDLC). By doing so, they implemented prototyping and iterative development into the otherwise linear

ADDIE structure. Nowadays, it's a technique often referred to as AGILE. At the time that they adopted this technique, the AGILE concept was still in its infancy and not often applied to training development. What the software development methodology did offer was the concept of lots of unit testing and lots of user testing, combined with a cross-functional team approach using experts instead of generalists. This is fundamental in software development—where systems architecture, database design, programming, user interface design, etc.—each require unique skills to do it right, and it is my belief that it is fundamental in any learning solutions development.

Let's look at some of the key attributes to the processes used by this company. First, there is a very detailed and rigid design process. The resulting design document is a full blueprint of the training program, without the actual content. I've seen design documents from companies that are upwards of 60 pages. A great deal of thought is put into the actual design of the instruction, the optimal way that we feel that this learning audience will be able to retain the information and demonstrate performance. This is not the same thing as a design document that focuses exclusively on what content will be included and the sequence of that content. Obviously, these are elements within a design document, but it is not the point of a design. This company then uses an iterative style of content drafting and review that is quite unique. I've discussed this approach earlier.

Instead of drafting entire course and then conducting a formal review of the subject matter expert, they develop the content in small chunks with reviews by the subject matter expert on an ongoing basis. They demand much from their subject matter experts, but they get away with it because the quality is exceptional and consistent. Subject matter experts have often claimed that it was much more work than they expected, but they enjoyed the experience and the result. So instead of reviewing the entire course at one time, this company may ask the subject matter expert to review a 300-word passage, the script for a media object, or the questions and answers for knowledge checks. When asking for new content, they will also request it in chunks, perhaps an authentic scenario for a instructional scenario, or some good distracters for practice questions, and of course to help fill in the gaps of the content. This content may be delivered by the subject matter expert in the form of a simple Word document or even an interview on the phone with the development team, which is sometimes quicker for everyone.

This iterative back and forth between the team and the subject matter expert creates a great deal of collaboration and ownership on both sides, which is fundamental to the success of the overall project experience. This company also staffs their cross-functional team with writers who are adept at online development, meaning they understand HTML and some of the more common authoring systems. After the initial review of chunks of content with a subject matter expert, these chunks of content are put online into the course. After the first set of reviews, all reviews thereafter are conducted online. This produces exceptional efficiency and eliminates most paper-based reports, but what might be the most important benefit of this online review is that it enables the client to fully <u>visualize</u> the final product. This is exceptionally important for a client, stakeholder, or subject matter expert who has never built an online course. I would add that it is even more important for a client who has never seen a "good" online course. It's exceptionally important that the client be able to visualize the final product.

In building a home, the architect will always produce an artist's rendition of the final house, but it's not until the house has actually been framed and the client can walk through the house that they are able to <u>visualize</u> the final product. It is at that time where any errors in the blueprint in the initial design are first recognized, and as construction continues, the refinements that will take the product *from good to great* are identified, and done so early enough that they can be safely implemented. Once the house is complete, it is very challenging to eliminate a wall or even move an outlet, but in the early stages of construction, these are easy changes. The scenario holds true for training development. The sooner the client can see the course, the sooner they can visualize the end result, and the sooner they can start to identify those items that are missing or can take the product from good to great.

GLOBAL INTEGRATION

Finally, the age of global development is upon us. Either because the audience itself is global or because the client and training development provider have decided to use global resources to reduce cost in today's industry, the involvement and influence of global staff is reality. So the process question is: How are these global teams integrated? I have noted many times that I do not believe in assembly line works; therefore, I do not believe that a domestic team can script everything on paper and send it to a offshore team and expect an effective result, every time. Instead, this global team must be integrated. A black box situation, where the provider sends it in and it comes back the next day by some random staff person in another country, is not effective. A collaborative situation where there is a dedicated individual in the country who is involved with your project from day one, and continues to stay involved by tightly collaborating with the project team, can be effective regardless of the role.

Some of the scenarios where I have seen effective use of global staff are in the use of in-tact teams, where all the resources necessary for the training developments are located in one spot offshore. This would include the instructional designer, the content writer, and media developer. In this scenario, most often the projects sent to this offshore team tend to be the less complex projects. Perhaps the subject matter itself is fairly well defined, such as the functionality of software or the standard operating procedures within manufacturing or even perhaps new product information. It is less likely that a highly complex topic, such as a leadership skill or new branding strategy or an initiative that is under development simultaneous with the training, will be sent offshore. What's the primary differentiator? It's the level of collaboration required to refine the content. If the content is already well defined, then I would suggest *any* decentralized team is more likely to be effective. If the content is not well defined, is more obscure, intangible, or aligned with an initiative that is currently in process, and a tightly collaborative team between development provider and the client is essential, then usage of a global team will be much more challenging.

I have seen scenarios where they try to relegate the global team to simply create the media development, but I've rarely seen when that has added any efficiency or cost savings. Why? Because the level of detail required by the high-priced instructional designer to draft and script the media objects, communicate those to the offshore resource, and review and correct the results that come back, are more labor-intensive than if the individual media developer was sitting next to the instructional designer, where the detail drafting is not required and a storyboard is not required. That seems obvious. In today's outsourcing environment, the pace of work that a development vendor must attain and where the client is often demanding is simply too fast for a decentralized team, especially on a global basis.

THE FINAL QUESTION

So the very important question for you to ask a vendor is: How does your process facilitate the use of global staff?

To summarize, here are the key questions that you are trying to answer in the Process Attribute:

- Do they use an assembly line approach or an iterative development process (such as AGILE)?
- Do they develop their online courseware (web-based, mobile, etc.) in an online environment or on paper-based storyboards?
- What are their drafting and review processes? Are they SME-friendly; do they utilize processes that are conducive to the SME's time availability?
- Do they enable online reviews of the online courseware while it is under development?
- Do they do user testing? Are their Alpha, Beta, and/or Pilot reviews of online courseware in an online environment for users, or are they paper-based SME reviews?

- Do they provide for flexibility in the process and timelines? Given that everyone is busy, time commitments vary, and priorities often change, how does their process adapt to these changes?
- What roles are involved in the process? Do they use one core ID to do all the design and development, or do they employ a team of multiple staff with different roles/expertise?
- How do they integrate their offshore staff (if used)? Do they offshore specific tasks, the whole project, or does it vary? What review process do they use for offshore work?

Chapter 7

Attribute #5: Technology

What do human resource professionals, sales professionals, manufacturing, and accountants all have in common? They each have an enterprise resource planning (ERP) system that allows them to integrate their workflow: do their jobs, share data across the organization, and do so in a manner that keeps things consistent and accurate. For a modest investment, they can automate and standardize their whole organization. For learning solutions development, we do not have such a system. Most L&D organizations create their own custom spreadsheets, use project management software, or possibly customize a database if they have the budget and resources to do so. However, the issue is that, without an integrated technology platform or some other combination of tools that facilitate the design, development, and collaboration, it is very difficult to run an efficient and highly effective development operation.

Imagine a situation where, at the touch of a button, you could see the status of every project in your portfolio. Imagine that, as a development provider, you could look at every development site and every client in order to recognize the financial performance and assess the quality of the product being produced, and then imagine that, as a buyer and client, you can likewise see the status and quality of every product under development, by every vendor working with you. Imagine that, with a touch of a button, you can see how your resources are being used, who is busy, who has time, where you have capacity for new projects, and the groups that need reinforcement to withstand their demands. Now imagine that the buyer and provider both have access to the same data and the ability to review the current status and deliverables of every project in their portfolio. Wouldn't that be divine?

> On a side note, my answer to this question was, "Yes, that would be divine!" but I also recognized that there was not an ERP product designed for the learning industry. So, I set out to build one and in 2013 launched Quantum7 and the QuantumConnect Development Management System, or DMS.

DECLARING A WAR ON SPREADSHEETS

This is extremely more important for a consulting organization or any development-outsourcing provider where the profit margins on a typical training development project tend to be fairly thin and thus poor project management could have a disastrous effect on the finances of the project, or possibly the finances of the entire company. It is exceptionally important for them to ensure that all their projects are on time and on budget, as well as their ability to ensure the highest utilization possible for their staff. A high utilization means lower overhead, a lower utilization means higher costs. Therefore, it's extremely important for them to be able to achieve their optimal balance.

The horror stories abound in the L&D industry. The most common scenario I have seen, meaning the vast majority of the organizations I witnessed, is one in which each training group, which may be a line of business within a corporation or an account team within a provider, has their own set of spreadsheets and their own processes that they follow. These spreadsheets are not integrated together in any particular way, not with each other or with the company's time tracking system. The results are job opportunities for highly compensated project managers who go from person to person and spreadsheet to spreadsheet to aggregate information to get any meaningful results regarding the current financial status of the project, with marginally few are able to determine the financial status of their overall operations. Those are the scenarios in a staggeringly large number of buyer and provider organizations.

A TOOL FOR EVERYTHING, EXCEPT WHAT WE NEED MOST

The common toolsets available right now, where most of the focus is being spent in the training industry, are the products that support the *creation* of the learning solutions, authoring tools, and those technologies used to *deliver* these solutions—learning management systems. There is a plethora of these tools, and the competition becomes fiercer as the potential of our technology continues to advance at light speed. This includes opportunities introduced by mobile learning, social networking tools, TinCan, and the conversion of our entire industry HTML 5 and other platforms. From a technical standpoint, the L&D **industry is actually a very exciting place to be right now.** When it comes to new and innovative ways to create products and deliver them to our learners, we couldn't have picked a better time. Believe it or not, the technology is the easy part. The technology has always been the easy part of e-learning. Getting your team to use the same authoring system and toolsets for building courses achieves a *singular objective* for your organization: preparing it. However, it doesn't address how these tools will be applied day-to-day to get the work done or how you manage the overall operations. Why should you care as a buyer? Because if your vendor doesn't have a strong toolset to manage the work and coordinate the many activities, then they will make up for that with highly compensated project managers, which leads to either higher costs or less of the costs directed to the actual development team.

In many of the outsourcing providers I have witnessed, there is still a strong reliance on spreadsheets to record data and make it available to the team and to their account leadership. The problem is getting the data into the spreadsheets and integrating all these spreadsheets across their enterprise. For any development provider with a time tracking system, adding this information to spreadsheets is a complex and redundant exercise. Either you have a master that each of the staff accesses to enter their own time, or the project manager is collecting the time sheets from all the employees and entering it into a master spreadsheet. It's highly inefficient. The vendors I have seen that have been more effective are those with a time tracking system where each employee can indicate the project and the task they are completing and the number of hours they spent each day. This data is then all aggregated in a database that enables the project managers and leaders to see how much time is being spent on each project, and when implemented exceptionally well, it enables them to compare those numbers with the original budget and determine whether the project is on track. It sounds obvious, but it's not being done by the majority of the corporations and providers I've encountered.

HIDDEN COSTS. INCREASED OVERHEAD.

Here's the hidden cost. If your provider does not have a toolset of this nature—if your provider is relying solely on the aggregation of spreadsheets by the project managers—then they are most certainly spending more money on project management than the company that has integrated tools. There are two adverse results to this scenario. First, as a client, when you write a check for the development of a training program, you want as many of those dollars as possible to go into the development and

quality of that program. If you are working with a vendor that does not have an adequate toolset and is managing all their projects manually, then you are spending a disproportional amount of your dollars on project management tasks that do not contribute the quality of the program.

Secondly, as the provider, all the additional time that you must spend manually tracking your projects and aggregating data increases the investment that you make in project management. It does not inherently reduce the amount of work required to build the training and complete each project. In other words, the client has paid you x-dollars for a training program, and it will require y-dollars of labor to complete the work. Now if your dollars plus your project management costs exceed those x-dollars, then that's when you lose money. To the extent that you can reduce your project management costs, your margin increases. Period! Thus, you're more likely to achieve success from a financial standpoint with solid technology.

EMERGENCE OF THE DMS

Note that it is not entirely the fault of the development providers that they do not have an integrated toolset. Until very recently, the L&D industry did not have the attention of software development companies who have built solutions for other industries. Unless the provider has the budget, ability, and foresight to build their own solution, they were forced to piece

144

together a solution from existing tools. That all changed in 2013 when the first **Development Management System (DMS)** was introduced by Quantum7 to the L&D industry. This DMS is sure to be the spark the industry has needed to introduce a new series of ERP functionality that is focused on the L&D processes to make the development more efficient and the providers more successful.

Within training development, there are lots of moving parts. We just mentioned project management. That's a big one. There's also financial management, the ability to roll up all the project information into one consolidated financial statement, with a high reliability as to the accuracy of that information. There is the workflow: what needs to be done, who's going to do it, when it is due, and how many hours a day you have to do it. There is the very important requirement for version control. There are lots of documents floating between the project team members and the subject matter expert—for example, drafts of content, drafts of design documents, drafts of media scripts. Each time someone receives a document and makes changes, those revisions need to be tracked and the team needs to ensure that they do not accidentally overwrite the most recent version. I mentioned earlier that the highly effective organizations are those that do real user testing, so the ability to deliver the course online and track the comments from the users is also important. The bottom line is that there are lots of things going on and without the proper toolset, each of these things adds to the labor requirements and the time requirement to do the basic tasks. A highly effective development vendor has a toolset that facilitates many of these activities, and these providers are going to be more efficient, more profitable, and better partners.

THE TOOLS REQUIRED

So what are some of the tools and technology solutions to expect from your vendor? Perhaps the easiest way to answer that question is to walk through the default process—the standard methods that we use to go about developing learning solutions and executing projects. First, you need to be able to request the project. Now, if you're working with a vendor on individual projects, one at a time, then this is not an area where technologies can benefit you much, but if you are outsourcing an entire department, a division, a large consistent volume of courseware, then this is where a convenient tool can help both the vendor and yourself. There should be an easy way for you to submit a request and for the vendor to estimate the cost of that request. The key feature of such a tool would be to ensure that your request does not *fall through cracks* and that your vendor is able to aggregate all the requests, determine their capacity to fulfill them, in which order, and how soon. It doesn't have to be high tech. I have seen organizations that use a standard template spreadsheet to submit requests and complete the estimates, and then aggregate them manually into a master spreadsheet. I witnessed a $5 million annual account use such a technique, and do so rather effectively. A more robust solution would be an online system where the client could complete a form and submit it to the vendor and allow the database to aggregate the data. The sophistication of the technology is not what's most important. What is most important is that your vendor **has** a solution and can communicate and implement that solution for your needs.

PROJECT PLANNING

So what's next? After the request is received and the budget is approved, the project team typically progresses by developing an initial **project plan.** I have seen highly successful operations that use detailed project plans, such as those that you might produce with Microsoft Project, but I have also seen highly successful operations that use a simple spreadsheet to communicate the plan. In this case, it's not the tool that matters. My personal view is that regardless of which tool they are using, there must be a *reasonable* amount of detail within the project plan. For example, if you have a training development project that is going to last 10 to 14 weeks, and it has a project team that consists of two to four people, and you're going to produce a single course in a single subject matter, then you do not need a complex Gant chart that has 64 steps.

One of the most highly effective vendors I've witnessed used a one-page spreadsheet for every project plan. It looked like a calendar; five primary columns, one for each day, and one row for each week. Each milestone date was color coded to indicate the owner of the task: ID, media, technical, client, etc. The plan was always sized to a single 8.5x11" piece of paper no matter how long the project (within reason). That provided a detailed plan in a format that the client was familiar with: a calendar. It also provided a very effective model for addressing the inevitable date shifts. The client is always busy, no matter how emotionally dedicated, and *things happen*, dates need to shift—a day here and day there—but the calendar spreadsheet made it very easy to communicate the domino effect. It was very clear to the client that if one cell needed to move, then the subsequent cells may likely move. Regardless of the sophistication of a Gant chart, it's not nearly as effective at communicating that message to the client.

I'm not going to get into the details of effective project management in this book, but it is reasonable to expect that the vendor will assemble a plan of attack, in whatever format, that guides the team effectively without over architecting the plans and undue overhead.

PRODUCTION MANAGEMENT

So let's get back to the project as we are now underway. A highly effective development vendor will have the ability to efficiently aggregate their project plans and the key information about the labor, budget, employees involved. This cannot be solved with a series of spreadsheets; where there is a spreadsheet for every project, the labor hours are manually entered, and the aggregation of all the projects is a manual process.

When I started my former company, Option Six, and we had 10 to 12 employees working on 8 to 10 projects at one time, we started with the typical solution of using a spreadsheet to track all those projects, the people assigned to those projects, and the hours that they worked. I very quickly identified this was a highly inefficient process due to the manual tasks involved. I was spending way too much time tracking the data, and as a start-up, I wasn't about to pay a project manager $50,000 to do it for me. Moreover, the spreadsheets were not giving us the detail that we needed to efficiently manage the budget for each project, effectively predict the outcome of each project, and determine our ability to handle future projects.

Stated differently, there is no substitute for the efficiency of project plans that are automatically updated when the staff enters their hours worked. There's no replacing a single screen that shows you a view of the entire portfolio of your organization, the current status and health of the projects, the ability to track the data down to specific milestones instead of one high-level budget status, and the ability to predict the outcome of a project *before there's a problem* and balance the capacity of your operations. Any system that provides this functionality is invaluable to a vendor. It ensures that they can efficiently respond to your needs and make a profit in the process. As I stated many times, that's a formula for success. Without an effective system of this nature, too much overhead is generated tracking the business and too many unknowns are possible that will jeopardize profitability. I am aware of only a few development vendors that uniformly deploy such a system. I witnessed one larger provider who had no indication of the profitability of any project, until the project was finally over. I believe the time has arrived when it will become an essential part of any practice and a key criterion for selecting your vendors. It's with that prediction that I am thankful that the DMS has arrived to the L&D market.

DRAFT AND REVIEW

So you have a project plan and your team in place, and now **it's time to get to work.** During the actual development of the course, there are two primary tasks that can be executed efficiently and effectively with the aid of the right technology. The first task is the content draft and review process, which would include the drafting and reviewing of initial documents such as design documents, then the subsequent draft and review of all content, media, etc. The second task, specific to online courseware, is the development of the course in the online environment, which includes the capabilities of the team to develop the online course themselves without the usage of external programmers to do so.

So let's address the **content draft and review process.** The actual drafting of the content is not, in my experience, a task that needs to be over-engineered. The basic tools such as Microsoft Word are certainly effective, but require a disciplined version control process to ensure that all the edits received from your subject matter expert are incorporated. This requires a very disciplined file management process and naming convention to ensure that you have an effective version control of the files themselves, a means to quickly identify the most recent version of a document and to archive previous versions. This latter part can be effectively managed, with discipline, and the basic file manager on a Windows server or other file management server, or you can deploy something similar to Share Point or even some LCMS systems that enable you to use them as a repository for documents. You should be able to assume that most training development providers have evolved an effective measure to make sure that they have efficient file management and version control, but it's very important to ask them how they do it.

Fundamental in the draft and review process is the means by which the reviewers, subject matter experts, or other stakeholders access the latest version of the drafts; this includes final versions of design documents, content, storyboards, and other formal documents where an official approval is necessary. **This is where the process gets tricky.** The typical means of sharing drafts and documents between the team and the client is via email. Some effective file management systems enable you to email a link to the document, thereby ensuring that the client is seeing the most recent revisions. The problem with email attachments is simply ensuring that the attachment you're working on is the most recent version. Failure to do so merely gobbles up the editorial process and risks important changes *falling through the cracks.* Some of the highly effective development vendors I have seen have an online portal where the client can access the most current deliverables. This ensures that every document they are accessing through the portal is the most recent version. To that end, the most important features of the review process and its supporting tools are the ease of access to the most recent documents and disciplined version control.

ONLINE DEVELOPMENT

Now let's talk about the **development** of the online course. This is an area where I tend to disagree with the manner that a very large majority of the development vendors develop their online courses. The standard process is that the instructional designer writes all the content and drafts the online course using paper-based storyboards. Thus, the reviewers are reviewing an online course on paper, not the ultimate format of the program itself. The standard process then continues to the Alpha test, when the subject matter experts review the full storyboard, and again all the changes are made on paper. The standard process then typically migrates to the conversion of the paper-based course into an online environment by a team of external programmers located either domestically or offshore. The online version is then reviewed by the SMEs in what they call a Beta test. Any changes to the Beta are again sent to the programmers to produce a final version. This tends to be the standard process and one that I find highly inefficient. There is a better approach. I refer to it as an online process for an online product.

In my experience, the faster you can get an online course in front of your client, the more likely you are to produce a highly effective program. The ultimate delivery mechanism for an online course is not paper; it's an online interactive program. This cannot be simulated by paper storyboards or PowerPoint presentations. An online course should be an immersive experience, not simply a presentation of content that resembles a presentation. If your only method of reviewing an online course is on paper, you'll most likely end up with a course that looks like a presentation. If you want to produce an engaging learning experience, then you need to be able to develop the course in its ultimate format, using an online development environment.

Plus, you have the very real situation, which I addressed in the Process Attribute section, where the subject matter experts will *rethink* the content when they see the content online. This is true for any subject matter expert who is building the first online course and is even true for instructors who has been teaching the course for many years in a classroom environment. They do not have the experience to realize the potential for the training program until they see it firsthand. Converting a linear classroom course into an online course requires more than just putting the slides and lecture online. To create an effective online learning program, you must be able to create a new learning dynamic to replace the dynamics commonly found in a classroom. This is often when the really creative development of the course occurs.

The highly effective vendors are those where the online development is done by the project team during the draft and review process. Once the subject matter expert has provided the initial content for the first review in document format, that content should then be put into the online environment. (This goes without saying that the online interface for this training program should have already been agreed upon at this point.) Any subsequent reviews of that content should be conducted in the online environment. This is the only way to ensure a highly effective online course. Stated plainly, it is an online process for an online product. If the course is being developed entirely on paper, then you are handcuffing the process. So the question for your vendor is, who's doing the online development, what tools are they using, and when will it be available for review?

USER TESTING. FEEDBACK CONSOLIDATION

This brings us to the next phase of the project and to me the most fundamental in ensuring that the course is instructionally effective. I'm talking about the **user test**. An instructional designer and a subject matter expert can work very effectively together to create a learning experience that is "accurate," but that does not mean that it is an effective learning experience—meaning that the learners will garner the skills intended that will achieve the performance level required to meet the business objective. The instructional designer and the subject matter expert cannot make this assessment. Only the actual employees who will be taking the course can. The highly effective vendors I have seen conducted a user test at the Alpha stage and again at the Beta stage (typically three to six employees is enough). The course does not have to be 100-percent complete to have an effective user test. In fact, the expectation should be plainly made to the employees taking the course that it is not only "incomplete," but the whole point of the review is to gain their input that can be incorporated into the final product. The user testers will respect this knowing that they will be able to make a contribution to the effectiveness of the course. I guarantee it. I've seen it thousands of times. You will produce a better product. The combination of the instructional designer and the SME, with the input and validation by the learners, can guarantee a highly effective learning experience. The vendors with the means of

155

developing the courseware online, during development, and delivering an online version for the client's employees will produce a more successful experience in the outsourcing relationship.

The second technically supported requirement for user testing is a method to collect the feedback comments, issues, suggestions, bugs, and so on from the reviewers. The vendor's technology should enable the users to review the training program and submit this feedback, while aggregating the comments from all users into a list that can be assessed by the development team. The more this process is supported by a system, the more efficient the process will be. If the vendor is relying on spreadsheets to collect the comments, then they are left with the daunting task of aggregating all the content comments together, making them consistent, then continuing with the manual process of assigning these tasks to be completed, and tracking that they have been done so. A vendor with a supporting technology should be able to allow the reviewer to enter their comments at any point during their review, have all those comments aggregated into a consolidated list online, where comments can be categorized and assigned to the individual who will be making the changes.

This functionality should also support the interim step where the development team is able to produce a report of all the comments and review this with the client. Some of the comments may require obvious changes, such as a misspelling or a media object that crashes—something obvious. However, there may be other comments that require some discussion. Some may simply be preferential to a particular user, and the client decides to reject the comment. Some of the comments may introduce debate over specific areas of the content, whether it's being addressed effectively, whether it's accurately reflecting the future state of the content, anything that requires a discussion with the subject matter expert. This review process tends to be highly productive and continuously engages the client in the development process. Plus, it's emotionally beneficial to both the team and the client to hear what the learners think about their hard work. With an effective technology, the vendor can process all the comments and ensure that none of the comments *fall through the cracks*. This is essential for a positive client experience because nobody wants to be in a situation where the final product is rolled out, and then an error is discovered or an omission is discovered after the fact.

THE LMS AND LCMS

The final stage of the project is the integration with the client's technical environment. Most frequently, the client will be using an LMS to support their online courses. Anyone who has been in the training development industry for more than a couple years is well aware of the SCORM requirements (or AICC). A training development vendor who is building their course online using this formal protocol should be able to seamlessly deliver the final product for integration into the client's LMS.

Frankly, this really is the easy part. At the end of the day, the delivery mechanism is totally irrelevant to the *effectiveness* of the instruction itself. It is simply a requirement to effectively deliver the instruction to the audience. In my opinion, this should be "a given" in a relationship with any vendor. For clients who do not use a standard LMS or hosting the courses on a standard web server, it is very important that you are choosing a vendor who is savvy enough to help you with the final integration. This includes many smaller companies who do not own an LMS. In my former companies, I had some very well-known clients who had very small training departments and budgets. The implementation of an LMS was cost prohibitive, so we would help them, using their existing technology, to produce a solution that did the basics that they would need. Nowadays, there are several widely available and free LMS solutions that could be considered. The bottom line is to select a vendor who's technically savvy enough to help you with these decisions and **seamless integration with the final solution.**

The obvious omissions here are the content authoring systems and LCMS used by the client. Certainly, it would be preferential to find a vendor who is already well versed in your content authoring system and usage of your LCMS. Each of these tools has a place in the process. I'm not partial to any of them. I've seen companies find a solid role for an LCMS, but I'm also seen many companies buy-in to reusability promises of the LCMS sales team, yet fall way short on the actual usage of the tools. You should expect that your vendor can use your existing toolset, or integrate their own toolset, to produce interim online versions of the course throughout the development process and facilitate online user tests.

DON'T DISMISS THE VENDOR'S TOOLSET

If the client has already standardized on a content authoring system or LCMS, then does the vendor need to use this system during development? You would expect the development team to produce a final product that conforms to your environment, but must they use it day to day? What do I mean by that? Recall that you selected your vendor because you believe they are the best at what they do—at least at the price you can afford. That implies they have spent years refining their practice, their processes, and how they do their work. Forcing them to drop their current toolset and processes to adopt yours is instantly going to produce inefficiencies. You would not be leveraging the highest capability of their team. This is not cheating the system; you have your standards, but a very efficient workaround is to allow the provider to leverage their best practices while still delivering a final product that is compatible with the client environment.

The provider will use their existing tools to develop and user test the online course, and then port it to the client's authoring system once they have achieved a near-complete status.

Let me elaborate on why I think using the vendor's tools is an "efficient" solution. The first objective for both the client and the vendor is that the resulting product will produce the necessary performance of the audience. Second, it must work in your environment (and perhaps a good third objective is that it was completed on time and on budget). As long as these objectives are achieved, you must give your vendor leeway. Let me give you an example. Several years ago, I was fortunate to win a very large multiyear, multimillion dollar account with the largest company in its industry sector. The contract was for a very large volume of training programs that would be developed every year. While the client did their best to produce a forecast, the courses often would come without warning, and *time was of the essence* with nearly all of them. For anyone who has been around our industry long enough, this is a common occurrence no matter how hard everyone tries to be proactive. It's just the nature of business and the fact that the training business is downstream from *everything* that occurs in your business.

Our team was selected because they assessed that we were the best provider matched to their specific needs. Our organization was ten years old at the time and had spent considerable investment honing, fine tuning, and perfecting (to the best of our ability) our processes and our existing tools. We had plenty of awards and satisfied clients to affirm that we were getting it right. However, for any client to look at our organization and say "We think you're the best out there," but then expect us to change everything about the way we do our work would have been an absurdity. Instead, this new client welcomed our processes. They enabled us to produce courses for them with the efficiency and effectiveness that we had provided our other clients. Once complete, tested, and approved, we ported the final product into their standard courseware environment, Lectora. In short, for a training program that may have a 300-hour budget for development, we would spend 280 hours of that developing the learning experience with 20 hours reserved for the individual who converted the final product into Lectora. That was a highly efficient solution that took advantage of our capabilities and our backend workflow technologies, yet produced the product in the toolset the client required.

The case that I noted above is similar to a case where we developed large volumes of courseware for one of the top five pharmaceutical companies. We worked in collaboration with them to come up with a standard within the LCMS course interfaces that would meet their needs while allowing us to adapt to our existing processes. In this case, we developed courseware for this client for many years quite successfully, so we became a partner in the implementation of the LCMS. Like the case above, we developed the courseware using our processes and our tools that had made us so successful, and then imported the final product to the LCMS in the agreed-upon format. Everyone was happy.

REINFORCING TECHNOLOGY WITH PROCESS

Let me give you an example of an organization I encountered that was very successful. They did <u>not</u> have a fully *integrated* toolset. However, they did have a suite of disaggregated applications focused on each primary function in their process: project management, user testing, issues tracking, workflow, etc. These tools were tightly integrated into a refined process that enabled the tools and processes to work very well together, even though the data itself was not shared among the applications. For example, they had an application that allowed them to track all the projects in the portfolio across the entire company, and across all clients in an integrated manner, so that the time sheets from each individual and the project plans from each manager rolled into one system. This enabled the leaders of the company, everyone from the CEO down to each project manager, the ability to instantly see the status of any project, how it was doing on time, how it was doing on budget, and how the whole thing rolled out to the overall financial health of the operation.

They had a second application that they used for user testing that would deliver the course online and provide an integrated form for the users to provide feedback. These two systems were not integrated, but without stating the obvious, integrating the project management data with user test results isn't necessarily that critical. The user test system allowed them to load any deliverable, perhaps a design document or a Word-based module, but moreover, load a version of the online courses. Then they could enable the client to access that deliverable, review and make comments, and record all those comments into a central repository that they could then categorize, sort, discuss, assign, track completion, etc. These two tools alone made this organization exceptionally effective because project administration was seamlessly built into the process. In fact, they had very few project managers. Most of the project teams manage themselves with the system. The instructional designers drove each of the projects, and the project managers focused on load balancing. They were able to do online user testing with an integrated tracking system that really directed the workflow once testing process began. Those two systems gave them a tremendous competitive advantage.

They had other systems such as a manifest system for organizing all the media objects under development, but many of their other processes were manual, such as the file management and version control processes. That worked just fine because all the processes were well integrated around the applications. They had a crack team of specialists, and they were very disciplined. There was an infrequent case of overriding a previous version, and of course, they had computer backup so they could always restore an old version. So this is a great example of a company with some pretty good toolsets and some very good processes that produces a very cohesive solution.

I came across another provider who had actually built from the ground up a toolkit that includes all these functionalities integrated together: project management, financial management, resource management, workflow, user testing, etc. They are all in one seamless platform. In fact, I was so impressed with the platform that I partnered with them and started a new company around it: Quantum7. Recognizing the need in the L&D industry for an integrated solution as described above, we leveraged this system to introduce the L&D industry's first Development Management System (DMS). But that's another story for another day.

The ultimate question for the buyer is whether the provider has a strong toolset that can reduce costs. The cost of doing lots of the manual processes is eliminated. The cost of doing lots of project management processes is eliminated. The overhead required to run the operation is reduced. That is exceptionally important. Obviously, to the provider, all these reductions in cost increase their margins and allow them to run a healthy business. To the buyer, the provider that can run more efficiently and lower its cost will be able to offer a more competitive fee structure.

THE FINAL QUESTION

To summarize, here are the key questions that you are trying to answer in the Technology Attribute:

- What technology do they have in place to manage their workflow: work assignment, file management, review management, issues tracking, comment tracking, etc.?
- What tools do they use for project management?
- Do they have a system other than MS Project or spreadsheets?
- Is it tied to their financial systems?
- How much of the budget of each project is used for project management?
- What technology do they use for course testing and issues tracking/resolution?
- What experience do they have with your toolset?

Chapter 8

Attribute #6: Talent

This is where the rubber meets the road. Many times throughout this book, I have discussed the problem with the *training industry* in terms of its overall talent. There isn't a standard educational requirement or a certification process by which any of us can assess the capabilities of the people in our industry. There are no CPA exams, CPE credits, CME credits; there's not even a Six Sigma program that will allow us to compare one instructional designer against another. We are in a very unique situation in that regard.

The Talent Attribute addresses the skills and capabilities of the individuals that will be assigned to the client projects. This includes the educational background and previous experience, how they developed in support of the employees assigned to your account, how they transfer best practices from one part of the organization to another that would be supporting you in your work, how they define the roles, and how they compose the project teams. And it includes the on-boarding process for new employees, some of which was discussed in the Infrastructure Attribute.

So if this is such an important attribute in our industry, then why is it the sixth attribute? Doesn't it seem that if talent is so direly important, it would be the first attribute? Well the answer is simple. If the vendor you are hiring does not have the experience you need, does not have a methodology that will guide the quality of their work, does not have efficient processes or effective technology to support the operation, cannot scale to your needs without sacrificing quality, then talent doesn't matter. The vendor can have the brightest people in the world working for them, but if they have no guidance, they have no tools to use, they don't have the right support from their organization, then they are not going to be very effective.

I have seen organizations with very highly educated individuals that did not perform as well compared to organizations with more modest hiring standards, but were more sophisticated with structure, process, tools, etc.

HAVE HIGH EXPECTATIONS. NO EXCEPTIONS.

Personally, while I was a provider, it was very important for me to have the best talent possible. My clients were entrusting me with some of their more important issues, so I needed to assign people that get the job done. My personal reputation was at stake, as was my business, so I made sure that I would hire people who are less likely to make mistakes and more likely to produce exceptional results. Therefore, for instructional designers, we required a master's degree for everyone. We even had several PhDs on our staff. No matter how experienced you were, if you did not have a master's in instructional design, then you were not allowed to wear that title in our organization. This gave us a distinct advantage over much of the competition that was willing to hire anyone with a bachelor's degree and a few years of training experience and then offer them to their clients as an instructional designer. I'm not saying that they were not talented. I'm saying that this was my standard within my company. And in an industry where there is the absence of a standard, I used the only gauge that I had.

I'll repeat the analogy I used earlier. If you are a corporation and you need to identify an auditor, there are certain criteria that you would expect. You would expect that they would have a degree an accounting, have passed their CPA exam, and have experience in the industry that you serve. You most certainly would not hire someone simply because they understood QuickBooks or managed their family hardware store. Yet, unfortunately, we don't apply the same type of scrutiny on a consistent basis in the *training industry*. Now, part of this is that there is a shortage of *classically trained* instructional designers. There are only a handful of academic programs and many of them are master's degree programs that are not traditionally convenient to everyone. Therefore, we are in a situation where we have the difficult challenge of assessing the few variables available to us to determine whether an individual can effectively perform as an instructional designer. In the

Methodology Attribute, we discussed the characteristics I think are most crucial within instructional design. The challenge of finding someone who has the educational background, the relative experience in both adult education in a corporate setting, and a sound grasp on the instructional design methodologies are the significant ones that face the leader of any training organization.

All that said, if you are talking about hiring a vendor to develop your training and you plan to outsource projects that are very important to you—crucial to effectively conducting your business and where multiple stakeholders are counting on you to do it effectively—then you *indeed* should have very high expectations of the talent provided by the vendor. I have seen too many examples where a large provider wins a large account with a large client, but then advertises for instructional designers who simply have a bachelor's degree in *something related to training*. This doesn't leave me with a very encouraging viewpoint. Unfortunately, I have been close enough to several of these accounts to watch the repercussions, where the client's needs were not met and the employees themselves were dissatisfied.

In one particular example, after the first year of a large outsourcing agreement, over 50 percent of the initial staff hired had to be replaced, either because they were not performing to standard and were dismissed or because they felt they were not adequately supported and stepped away. In this field with the complexities that we face and in the crucial state where the client has entrusted the vendor to support them in their business, there is very little room for hiring mistakes. As I stated earlier, in an industry that does not have a standard qualification for an instructional designer, we have to go with a few common denominators that we can count on, one of which is the education background.

RECRUITING

So let's talk about the recruiting process. The most fundamental aspect of recruiting is how **proactive** the vendor is in its assembly of a *stable* of qualified candidates that are available when needed. What we do in training development is complex. We have to address all types of learners, from accountants to sales reps, from leaders to front-line workers, from PhDs to high-school educated employees. We have to address a wide range of subject matter and often do so without any previous experience. We often address new business initiatives that are being defined *during* our development project and systems that are under development during our projects, both of which are expecting the training to be available **the day after** the initiative or the system is ready for launch. Our subject matter may include very intangible subjects such as leadership and negotiation, collaboration and communications, or it may include sensitive content such as compliance and workplace harassment. It may include sales skills training and customer product training. The list goes on. The message is that we deal with a wide range of content domains, each of which may require a different instructional approach to be effective with each specific audience. There's nothing easy about this.

So recruiting new instructional designers and the other talent required for training development takes time. Your development vendor should have a process in place where they are taking the time necessary, *in a proactive manner*, before you need them, to solicit and identify the ideal candidates, to negotiate their salary so they can be hired without jeopardizing the vendor's ability to earn a reasonable profit, to be pretested in areas that are essential, such as the use of certain media skills where their writing or editorial capabilities are taken into account, and to establish their availability in the lead time necessary for them to make a transition.

An organization that is not leveraging this lead time is at risk of being in a just-in-time staffing environment. The risk there is that they will not be able to identify the quality talent they need quickly enough, keeping in mind that when a client identifies and assigns a project, they typically wish to start *immediately*. A just-in-time recruiting environment often doesn't provide the vendor with the leverage to negotiate an equitable salary; thus, they are paying more than they need and it sacrifices their profit capabilities, and it does not provide the adequate lead time for on-boarding the staff or helping them understand how the vendor does the work and how to use the vendor's tools and processes. The end result is that the new talent has to rely on their own background and do the best they can. You've just selected a vendor because of their global reputation, and they've just assigned someone off the street. You expected better.

ORIENTATION AND TALENT DEVELOPMENT

So once a company has hired talented individuals, what's next? What does the vendor do to orient the new talent to their company and help them achieve the same level of competency as the rest of the people at the company? How do they ensure that they are following the same processes and effectively using the tools? Once they are through orientation and working on the job, what measures are put in place to continuously develop them as professionals?

Perhaps more importantly, what is the vendor doing to share the best practices and experiences across the organization so a project team that is pushing the edge of innovation and tackling complex problems at one end of the organization is sharing that information with all the other sites in the organization. What channels do they have in place so a project team on another end of the organization that is struggling to adapt to the client's upcoming needs may discover project teams on the other end of the organization who have already accomplished those needs and can share their insight and perhaps some of their talent. What is in place for that? They could be using something as simple as brown-bag luncheons, or they could be using something more sophisticated. It really doesn't matter. The question is, do they have anything at all?

Too often I've seen providers who had teams achieving amazing feats within one of their development groups, but then have other groups that couldn't complete a basic compliance course. In one example, a very large outsourcing provider won a contract with an industry-leading technology company. They were contracted to help produce a library of courses in leadership. This included packaged courses and custom developed courses. The vendor unfortunately did not have the knowledge sharing programs I've highlighted. So while they had several teams that had successfully produced leadership courses, the team assigned wasn't among them; they were mostly new staff and had no knowledge of the other programs. They struggled, starting from the ground up without the benefit of the other teams' lessons learned. Further, even the information about packaged solutions could not be shared across the company. During the negotiation with one leadership course provider, they discovered that the company already had a contract with the provider. The company had no established means of sharing knowledge across their company.

ONE SIZE FITS ALL OR SPECIALIST?

And in terms of talent, does the vendor deploy a team of specialists, or do they assign a single one-stop-shop instructional designer. We had this conversation earlier in the Process Attribute. My preference is the team over the individual. It's not always a fundamental requirement to deploy a cross-functional team, but here's where you have to ask that question. There are certainly circumstances where a single instructional designer is the preferred choice over a team. In my opinion, if a company needed a one-hour course on a marketing topic and they needed it in the next 12 weeks, it would be most efficient to assemble a team of specialists. However, if the client had a long string of work needs over a longer period of time, and what they wanted as a full-time resource instead of a project-based resource, then a single instructional designer may be the right solution. That said, the issues of media development and effective writing do not go away simply because the client *prefers* to have someone full-time, on-site in the queue. Nonetheless, there may be circumstances where a single individual is a better solution.

LOCATION, LOCATION, LOCATION

Where is the staff located? Are they in a central development center where the requirements that I outlined in the Infrastructure Attribute can be realized, such as mentoring opportunities and the ability to assimilate new employees into a group of experienced individuals, thus having more time to learn the job? Or are they working from home, in a decentralized fashion, and interacting with each other through virtual means? This is a very important question because the needs of the account may dictate which of these environments is likely to be most effective! You know by now that I prefer a centralized environment for development for all the reasons I've mentioned in earlier attributes. Many of the dynamics required to make the Seven Attributes effective are simply easier when everyone is under one roof. This is an important question to ask during the RFP process.

The location of the vendor can often have a huge impact on the talent. One of the times that I was able to thrive was with an organization that was located in a college town. There was a regular stream of graduates from the School of Education, Department of English, School of Journalism, usability sciences, Informatics, etc. The wide variety of talent that we needed to develop learning solutions, specifically online training, was readily available. The other advantage is that because they were new graduates and living in a low-cost college community, they tended to be more affordable than talent residing in a higher-cost metropolitan area. Where I saw some struggles was with the companies that were located in the large cities, who were forced to pay the higher wages, had to address long commuting times to get the employees in the office, which resulted in constant requests from employees to work from home instead of driving to work. And, where the company in the college town tended to have first choice on the new graduates, the company in the metropolitan area had to somewhat *settle* for the candidates who lived in that city or face the relocation costs or needs to work remotely—neither of which improve efficiency or profitability. This is an important consideration for buyers who, at first, prefer that the vendor have a local presence in their town. If this location puts the vendor in a situation where their costs are increased, then neither the client nor the vendor is on a course for "success." It is very uncommon for a buyer to pay more simply because the provider is located in their town. You should consider a hybrid solution where certain client-facing team members are located closer to the client while the remainder of the team is in a lower-cost location.

FREELANACERS

One of the more common approaches I have seen within some of the highly effective development vendors is the effective use of freelance contractors. We are in an industry where there are a meaningful percentage of the professionals who prefer to work on a freelance basis instead of as employees. Given the wide variability of the types of projects and subject matter, they tend to prefer freelance mode so they can pick and choose the projects that interest them. As an employee, they may not always have that luxury and may be assigned to projects simply because they are available at the time of need.

The benefits of the contractor from the vendor's perspective is that they are paid only for the work they do, in contrast to an employee who is paid a fixed salary whether they are busy or not. Often, the freelancer is willing to work for a fixed fee instead of hourly. This is another benefit to the vendor in that there is a fixed cost associated with the project, making it easier to manage the budget. As long as the vendor can maintain the scope so the freelancer is not expected to work an extraordinary amount of time over the original plan, then both sides benefit. In my previous company, there were many occasions where we paid a freelancer the agreed upon fixed fee, but in the end it required less time than expected. That was fine from both sides. They managed to earn more per hour than expected, so they're happy. And I still paid the amount that I expected to pay, thus making the profit I expected to make. (Certainly, as business leaders, we would always try to get the budget as close as possible.) The other benefit is that on occasion, the freelancer has to take more time than expected, and then there is not an argument over whether I need to increase the fixed fee. This is essential in our business, because the work we do is challenging and it is therefore challenging to calibrate the capability of freelancer ahead of time in a fixed fee arrangement. I do not have to pay extra for an individual who simply takes longer to do the job then someone of equal pay. We often use the term "lost in the weeds," where the instructional designer spends an extraordinary amount of time, debatably unproductive, trying to grasp the content and making decisions.

The freelancers are a great source of staff when you're in a variable environment. Having a good stable of freelancers allows you to react very quickly, bring many on board, who hopefully have worked on your projects in the past. We often refer to it as "try before you buy," where once we have a freelancer who has demonstrated their capabilities, we would bring them on as a full-time employee. In one organization that I experienced, every employee was expected to be a contractor first, and then work his or her way into actual employment.

From a client's perspective, you are entrusting your business to this vendor. You should have high expectations of the people they assign, and you should expect that they have provided the support and mechanisms to attract and develop the highest caliber professionals possible.

CULTURE

This is a good spot to talk about culture. The vendor's culture and the working environment that it has established can have a very strong bearing on the capabilities of the employees. A positive work environment tends to create happy energetic employees, who you would expect would be able to produce a more engaging client experience and better product. I think that's reasonable to assume. A company with a culture of what I used to call "thirst for knowledge" is very beneficial to an industry such as ours, where everything we do is based on knowledge—taking the knowledge from our subject matter experts and transforming that into a device that produces knowledge in our audience. A culture where professionals who thoroughly enjoy their trade and have the passion to dive into challenges and collaborate with their peers to come up with the best practices, and then analyze lessons learned, is a culture that would be very beneficial to the client. In contract, a culture that simply "feels like a job" would not attain these benefits. A culture that encourages risk and creativity and is found in a very relaxed and collegial environment will produce dividends.

THE FINAL QUESTION

To summarize, here are the key questions that you are trying to answer in the Talent Attribute:

- What are their qualifications? Do they have master's degrees or bachelor's degrees? Do they have experience developing training or just managing it?
- Does the staff assigned have experience handling the complexity of the business needs (subject matter) you will assign to them?

179

- Do they have an effective on-boarding program? Do the new employees receive training on their methodology and work processes?

- If they are centralized, do they have a mentorship program? If they are decentralized, how do they support the growth and performance of their employees?

- Do they use all-in-one instructional designers (with the possible exception of media production), or do they use teams of multiple people focused on specific roles?

- How do they support the on-going staff development? Do they have social learning programs? How do they share best practices across accounts?

- Are they a consulting company or a staffing company? Which does your company need?

Chapter 9

Attribute #7: Innovation

Several times within this book, I've used the comparison of accountants and architects with instructional designers to illustrate some of the weaknesses in the training industry. The qualification of talent in the work experience, tools, and establishing standards are a couple of areas where I highlighted that certain industries and professions have a very sound infrastructure compared to the environment that most learning and development professionals work within. Let's turn the table a bit and talk about an area where the training industry is still at a "disadvantage," but which provides much more opportunity and "fun." That's the final Attribute: *Innovation.*

Innovation is the degree to which the vendor you select will enable you to adopt new techniques and new technologies at a faster pace than you could on your own. Now, every vendor out there is going to *talk* about how innovative they are. Everyone is going to have a couple slides and stories to tell about the adoption of new technologies. This may include mobile, social, performance support systems, virtual, etc. The real challenge is determining the extent to which those stories are going to benefit you. I've witnessed many organizations that will bring in their "guru," who is an expert on innovation, but it will be, from client to client, the same guru every time. This person is booked 120 percent and, while he can *talk* a great deal, he is less likely to be able to help you. So it is fundamental in the vendor assessment to find ways to get deeper, beyond the dynamics personality of the guru and understand whether the innovation capabilities of your vendor will suit you directly.

Innovations in the area of architecture and construction come slowly. Occasionally, there are improvements in materials and tools, but they come gradually and rarely have an immediate impact on the industry as a whole. You certainly see examples of true masters in their field who will produce houses and buildings that are absolutely stellar in their appearance. And you certainly have examples of homebuilders in the tropics who can produce a house that will withstand any hurricane (as long as it stays above water). Likewise, there has not been much innovation in the area of accounting. Certainly, the rules change on a regular basis as the government adjusts the accounting policies, and there are situations where a particular audit client needs more scrutiny than others depending on its industry. But aside from the rule changes, accounting is not a discipline that faces demands for their clients for more innovative solutions. The training industry is a whole different world, one that continues to become more exciting.

Over the last decade, the advances in technology have been staggering. Items that we use daily and almost take for granted didn't even exist ten years ago. The iPod, which took the world by storm and reinvented the way we listen to music, has almost displaced itself with an iPhone that not only plays music, but enables you to communicate with the world. We have seen full technical lifecycles in just the last decade. As a result, in today's environment, we have so many more options for the development and delivery of "knowledge." The word "training" becomes less and less relevant to some of the solutions. Advances in mobile communications, handheld computing, social networking, integrated performance systems are all on the horizon; consider the introduction of heads-up display, which looks like science fiction today, but in five years, this could be an everyday part of your wardrobe.

ROOM TO EXPERIMENT

Unlike the relatively slow-moving professions, the training development world is facing a barrage of innovative opportunities. This is a mixed blessing. While it offers many options, it also poses many challenges, especially for vendors. Clients expect the providers in our industry to be at the forefront of their practice, to be on top of the latest innovations, and to be the thought leaders in new ways of adopting them. As of the writing of this book, the changes are arriving at such a fast pace that it is nearly impossible to keep up, but it produces a vision of a future state that is very exciting.

In trying to highlight failures and innovation, I face a bit of a paradox. As I will elaborate further in the definition and success stories, effective adoption of innovation requires "failure." To be highly successful in the adoption of new innovation, **you must have room to experiment,** to try new things, determine what works and what does not, and begin to assemble a plan for the adoption that provides a high probability of success. Without the opportunity to experiment and **fail safely,** you do put yourself at risk in that your first attempt, perhaps one that has a critical impact on the business, will not be successful and thus the reputation and the impression of the team responsible is dramatically harmed. So I find it difficult and almost unproductive to highlight examples where I've seen the attempted adoption of innovation as "a failure."

The one example of failure that I will highlight is when the attempt at innovation was driven by the supplier of the technology itself. No offense intended, but I have never seen the adoption of an LCMS achieve anywhere close to the potential promoted by its sales people. In addition, I have seen multiple attempts in the use of 3D technology that was promoted by the makers of 3D technology tools fail to achieve any business objective and wide-scale adoption of the audience that was initially advertised. My experience is broad, and I'm sure there have been successes, but I am not aware of them. I have seen some really fascinating tools that allow you to put together software simulations and run them in a just-in-time performance environment, but I have never seen one implemented as fast as the salespeople say it can be. So without beating this dead horse, I will simply leave a word of caution. Make sure that the person introducing the innovation to you has your best interests in mind, and not just theirs.

THE GURU

I will confess that, on more than one occasion, I was asked to stand up and talk about innovation and a particular new technology or technique that was being used in training development. I had enough base knowledge to present an informative perspective, but I was terrified that someone would actually ask me a question about it because I had never actually executed the innovation. Guilty as charged! Many of us in consulting have been forced to do so. That's not a problem for general understanding. I can stand toe-to-toe in a debate about the virtues of the innovation, but when establishing an outsourcing relationship, it is essential to make sure that you are talking to someone who *has* implemented the innovation and determine how/when they will be involved with your account. You must have the ability to talk directly to the experienced employees to verify that this company has indeed *executed* on the innovation, and not simply read about it.

So what are the things that you might look for? You might look at their image and reputation in the industry; are they attending and presenting at conferences, are they publishing white papers or books, are they sponsoring research and conducting webinars? These are a few easily accessible ways of revealing the depth of their innovation capability.

In addition to the "guru" and the company's experience, perhaps what is even more important is the vendor's **capacity** for experimentation. Now, this is something that is truly a fair measure of vendors and a way to establish a realistic expectation for your outsourcing relationship. Fundamentally, you cannot expect that the guru is going to be dedicated to your account and/or readily available at a moment's notice. It's just not possible. Gurus are most likely their highest performers and most requested talents. What you should be able to expect however is that this vendor will become a reliable "partner" throughout your innovation assessments and adoption process. You should be able to expect that they are as *energetically and aggressively* pursuing the adoption of innovations as you are. You should expect that they have set up some sort of (let's call it a) "lab," that allows them to install and play (for lack of a better word) with the new techniques and technologies. What you need most of all is ***room for error.*** You need space to try new things outside the context of a mission-critical project. If your first active attempt at introducing innovation is in the face of the mission-critical project, a big business initiative, then you have opened yourself up for **real failure** because you simply have not provided room for error. Let me characterize "failure" in this case: What it takes to be successful in the adoption of something new is room to try it and be able to fail, safely, without affecting your business. You must have time to work through the kinks and possibilities in advance so that when the opportunity emerges, these innovations can provide an outstanding solution.

Your vendor must be able to provide space and be a partner in the assessment and adoption of new innovations; in other words, they will provide people knowledgeable to help in the initial vision stages, help in the initial planning stages, and prepare for implementation. As the client, you may not always have a budget to spend on this phase; in fact, it's very unlikely that the client has a budget that they can use to "experiment." Therefore, you must find a vendor willing and able to pursue new innovations **because they are already doing so internally,** so they can be there as your partner when the time is right. This may sound like an unfair position for the vendor, but if they want to promote that they are capable in the adoption of innovation, then it is a fair expectation that they are preparing to do so *on their dime*, not yours.

ADOPTING INNOVATION

There are two ways to adopt innovation. The first is to select a high potential innovation and experiment with it for a while before you feel like you have enough understanding to successfully implement it in real time within your business. The second approach is to "damn the torpedoes," acquire the innovation, toss it out there, and work like mad to make it work. This may not be your first choice, but it is not always a bad option. Any organization that sticks out their heart and soul and dedicates themselves to the success of anything has a high potential for success. Allow me to give you an example. One of my company's clients is a large provider of home-improvement supplies. They wanted to adopt a mobile handheld device so that every employee had access to the latest product information and up-to-date training information and could support the customer at the point of need. They made the single largest purchase of Apple iPhones in history, sent it out to the business, and said "Figure it out." What resulted is one of the most efficient and innovative solutions that I've witnessed. They now have a situation where any store employee can bring up any information they need, standing right beside the customer, help the customer plan a project, identify the right materials, and do everything the customer needs with the click of a stylus. I worked with a very large pharmaceutical company that decided they were going to convert all their product training to handheld devices. The solution was in the planning stage for quite some time. It wasn't until their Japanese affiliate stated "All our training will be delivered on an iPad" that real progress happened, and it happened fast. Within a year, nearly all their product courses had been converted to a mobile platform.

Now, I tend to prefer the first method. I like the opportunity to determine how to get the most value out of an innovation before we try it. I also like the opportunity to work out the bugs, kinks, and scenarios we never imagined before committing something to a real business situation, where everyone's job is dependent on this innovation. Remember the 1990s when everyone was installing a new ERP system, and the number of failures that occurred—massive budget overruns, projects delayed by over a year, etc.? I remember them plainly. While the ERP technology was a valuable innovation and most companies strongly benefited once it was implemented, the process was often painful. I know the difference between a good analysis and "paralysis from analysis," but I think by giving you the space to experiment, you will not only reduce the risk of failure, but also identify additional opportunities that were not initially conceived.

The successful vendors I've witnessed, who have been able to consistently implement new innovations with their clients are those that have either selected a specific innovation and dedicated part of their organization to understanding and commercializing their expertise, or they have been able to afford to have one or more experts in their organization spearheading the evolution of their practice and have the ability to implement the innovation. Regarding the first organization, I have often stated that when outsourcing training development, even when you're looking to consolidate dozens of vendors down into a single provider, it is useful to keep a small set of boutique providers that offer specialized abilities. An organization that has dedicated a special part of their practice for, let's say, business simulations is much more qualified to help a client implement new leadership training that leverages simulations than a larger company that is serving all the other needs of the client, but has not used simulations in leadership training. The client would in essence be paying for the learning curve of the larger vendor versus benefiting from the deeper knowledge of the boutique. Likewise, the larger consulting organizations are often able to cost justify establishment of a new department or division focused on a specific innovation; for example, learning portals is a service line within one of the larger providers that I've been exposed to.

THE FINAL QUESTION

To summarize, here are the key questions that you are trying to answer in the Talent Attribute:

- Do they have experience in the emerging technologies and techniques?

- Do they have a team and/or reputation as thought-leaders? Do they have more than one thought-leader?
- Are they involved in the industry? Do they speak at conferences or publish?
- Do they have the internal infrastructure to test and experiment with new innovations? Can they help you adopt new ideas and tools?

Chapter 10

Great RFPs

Let's talk a little bit about the RFP process. It is my opinion that one of the best ways to understand the proposal process and really succeed in its execution is to look at the process from the *vendor's* point of view. If you understand how the vendors in our industry approach the RFP response process, it will provide you insight to be successful on your next one. How do the vendors decide which RFPs to respond to? How do they interpret the questions? What process do they follow? What challenges do they face? How can you make the process easier for the vendor and more effective for you?

Training development is one of the most frequently outsourced services, and for good reason. The typical training development project is transactional: assemble a team, build the course, and disperse. Certainly, it's more complex than that, but it's episodic nature makes outsourcing an easy rationale. Toss in a provider's added expertise and innovation, and you may end up with a formula that produces great returns. The key ingredient is finding the right provider, one who really fits your needs and can meet your expectations. Most often, you use the RFP process to identify that provider. It is then reasonable to conclude that the more effective the RFP process, the more successful your outsourcing initiative.

Over the last 13 years, I have been the lead on dozens of RFPs. These have ranged from small projects of $10,000-$100,000 to large multimillion dollar accounts that span multiple years. As I've said frequently, "I haven't seen it all, but I've seen a lot." I can tell you about the RFPs that I found very effective and enabled me to provide a solid response, whether we won or not. I can also tell you about the RFPs that were incomplete or ill-defined, constrained my ability to present ourselves, and (in my view) really did short-cut the client's ability to do a strong assessment of the vendors—the proposal where the vendors are left saying, "good luck." I'm not saying that because I may have lost some of those. We won our fair share of RFPs of this variety, so my insight is based more on the challenges we encountered after the win as a result of the incomplete proposal process.

There are two types of proposals. Some of them are small responses. These tend not to have a formal RFP. Instead, they are based more on the information gained during a one-hour phone interview. The result was not much more than 5-6 pages documenting our understanding and defining parameters of the projects. These are often one-off's, single projects to build one or more courses, and most likely there were only a couple vendors solicited. These are the easy proposals to write because (due to the phone call) you can create a personal interaction, dig deep to really understand the client's needs, and produce a response in a relatively short period of time. Throughout our industry, on any given day, there are hundreds of proposals at play that fit this scenario.

To produce a really effective proposal, the vendor needs to understand the client's needs. What problems are they trying to solve? What is their vision for success? Is this part of a larger initiative? What successes or failures have they had? Do they have current standards to be observed? And of course, the vendor wants ample time to provide a (focused) description of their ability specific to the client's needs. For small proposals, when we are able to have a conversation with the client, we are also able to uncover all the information that would make a difference in the project. Further, in a proposal, I want to be concise and yet complete. By the 10th year of my business, we had produced lots of great things for huge clients, but which ones are pertinent to your needs? You don't want me wasting time telling stories that are irrelevant, so the more I understand about your needs, the more focused my stories, experiences, demos, proposed solution, and so on will be. The proposals that began with a conversation rarely left any misinterpretation and provided the client specifically with what they needed.

The other RFPs are of the more formal variety. These are the proposals I want to spend the most time discussing because they

Seven Attributes Framework

are the most challenging and are often tied to the largest, most risky initiatives, including sole source outsourcing. The fundamental challenge of this proposal process is clearly communicating your needs to the vendor and giving the vendor enough flexibility to provide you with their strongest response. There are several solid ways to achieve this. I will discuss those. There are also several solid ways to shortchange the effort if you are not careful. I'll discuss those also.

Let's start with the basics. The larger proposals often have the following in common:

- A rigid timeline and due date
- Dozens of questions
- The opportunity to submit our own questions
- Sometimes a blind Q&A via conference call
- Sometimes a proposal submission system
- A "down selection" process
- Face-to-face presentations by those selected
- Lots of negotiations

So before we get into the actual contents of the RFP, let's explore some ways to improve your odds of success along the list above.

195

THE INSIDER'S PERSPECTIVE

So let's talk a little bit about the RFP process from the "provider's" perspective. I believe that the best way to understand the proposal process and really succeed in its execution is to look at the process from the provider's point of view.

How do the providers decide which RFPs to respond to? How do they interpret the questions? What process do they follow? What challenges do they face? How can you make the process easier for the vendor and thus more effective for you?

First and foremost, to produce a really effective proposal, the vendor needs to understand the client's needs. What problems are they trying to solve? What is their vision for success? Is this part of a larger initiative? What success or failures have they had? Do they have current standards to be observed? And of course, we want ample time to provide a (focused) description of our ability "specific to the client's needs."

Don't underestimate the complexity of your needs. There's nothing simple about training development. Your solicited providers may be responding to the need for software development courses by a technology company, clinical trials courses for a pharma company, sales courses for an automotive company, or compliance courses for an insurance company, all at the same time. I've been there. No matter what problem you're trying to solve, it is very unique to you.

In my view, this is the most important attribute of an effective RFP. How well can the buyer communicate their needs? The better your description is, the better my response will be. Personally, I have always preferred a conversation over any written description. It is easier for the buyer, no doubt, than writing volumes and trying to anticipate all the questions that I may have, but also allows the provider to really dive into the needs, asking questions that the buyer may not have considered. Within one hour, I can usually gather enough information to determine the best approach to the proposal response.

Unfortunately, the phone call isn't always permitted. In fact, it is quite frowned upon by many procurement professionals. I understand that they don't want the provider's sales reps pestering the key stakeholders, but some manner of a client interview will <u>always</u> increase the quality of the provider's response. Here's why.

When writing a proposal, I want to be concise and yet complete. I know the client doesn't want a dissertation and doesn't care about my career history. The buyer wants me to get to the point, but what point do they want? By the 10th year of my former business, Option Six, we had produced over 500 projects for huge clients (including the top company in the 10 largest industry sectors). We helped our clients solve major problems, roll out new projects, change their brand strategy, and expand into global regions, but which of these engagements are pertinent to **YOUR** needs? You don't want me wasting time telling stories that are irrelevant, and I certainly don't want to ignore a case that is perfect for you; the more I understand about your needs, the more focused my stories, experiences, demos, and proposed solution will be. The proposals that began with a conversation rarely left any misinterpretation, and we were able to provide the client specifically what they needed.

GIVE THEM TIME

Regarding the timeline and due date, be sure to **provide a fair and ample amount of time** for the vendors to reply. I have marveled at times with the RFPs that we would receive where the magnitude of their decision and the timeline just do not mesh. I've seen examples where the client has decided to outsource their entire T&D operations, and gave us three weeks to respond. It seems to me that if you are making that large leap, you'd want to spend *a little more time* on the proposal process to ensure that you have (a) solicited the right vendors and (b) provided them ample time to meet your needs.

I've heard the phrase, "Exercise the vendor." It is a practice used within procurement to determine just how badly the vendor wants the work. Contained within that tactic are very short timelines, due dates immediately after holidays, and other requirements that force the vendor to work longer hours and rush the job to meet the deadline. Two of the largest proposals I have ever written were due immediately after the Christmas holiday. The Q&A was due on Christmas Eve and the proposal due on January 2, forcing our team to work through the holiday period. It's a really bad way to start a relationship and achieves very little to benefit the client. The basis for establishing a highly effective development operation is a strong, trusted relationship. That starts with the proposal process. Keep in mind that *your* RFP is also your *first impression* to the client. You should want it to be a good one. We have walked away from RFPs in the past when it was clear by the nature of the response timeline that this would be a difficult client to work with.

> Do you really want to be friends and make a good first impression with your provider? Set a reasonable timeline, and then once the process begins, extend it by a couple days! As an insider, that's consistently been the best news we can receive.

YOUR RELATIONSHIP STARTS WITH THE RFP

The basis for establishing a highly effective development outsourcing operation is a strong, trusted relationship between the buyer and provider. That starts with the proposal process. Keep in mind that the *buyer's* RFP is also your *first impression* to the *provider*. You should want it to be a good one. We walked away from RFPs in the past when it was clear, by the nature of the response timeline, that this would be a difficult client with work with. On the contrary, I inquired who wrote the RFP after the formal presentation for one of the largest accounts that I won. I complemented them on the outstanding work. I wasn't pandering; I actually enjoyed writing that proposal. Fortunately, they returned the compliment about the proposal. I still believe it was some of my finest work. Many of the best practices from that RFP and my proposal are contained within my book. It was a great start to our relationship.

THE PROPOSAL PROCESS

So why do we need so much time? It would be insightful to know what goes on behind the scenes of a typical consulting organization during the preparation of a proposal. Let me set the stage.

First, we're already busy. Most provider organizations run thin. It's vital to making a reasonable profit and maintaining a strong business. That means everyone is already assigned to other clients. In addition, most of the small to mid-sized providers do not have dedicated proposal writers; when they do, these individuals tend to be more or less administrative roles and are not the industry experts who will end up writing the salient parts of your proposal. So, to produce an outstanding response, the provider first needs to free up the time by the right people.

The next part is to review the proposal. If we are required to use one of the proposal portals, like Ariba, then we need to download the RFP, dissect it into sections, and drop it into Word documents that are easier to edit. Oh, and another tip about proposal systems. The character limitations offer little value. I can't count the number of proposals where we spent *almost as much* time rewriting responses to fit within an arbitrary character limit as we did writing the original response. If you want to really know about my company's experience and the methodology we'll follow, then you need to allow plenty of room to tell that story. I understand that you don't want to read 90 pages, but I will counter that replacing your provider after you made the wrong choice will cost you even more time.

The next step is to assign each section to the best person to respond. Keep in mind that most providers, especially the large ones, will need to use multiple people to produce a complete response. The individual completing the financial portion may not be the same one completing the *About Your Company* section. The person describing our methodology or detailed the solution may not be the same person gathering the bios and determining the timelines. There are cases where one person does it all, especially at smaller providers. While I was at GP Strategies, I wrote two of the larger proposals in isolation, holed-up in my basement office, but I still needed to ping other people throughout the company to get the information required by the proposal: "Hey, can you send me a summary of the work you're currently doing for *so and so*; I have a RFP looking for the same thing." In another example, the buyer wanted to outsource their company's entire training development services. It was a monster. No fewer than 15 people were involved, and at two points, we all flew to a central location to collaborate.

Once each person has their assignment, we review to see if "we've written this before." After 13 years leading training development providers, I've answered many, many questions, but when and where? This is the first time-consuming part—deciding whether to spend time writing it again or trying to find the original? Personally, I find it surprising that, even when I find my old response, there's always something unique about the new proposal that requires me to revise the answer. The average proposal I've received has 30-50 questions. The two largest proposals I've written (both of which we, fortunately, won) were over 90 pages by the time they were complete. So the more past response I find to edit, the more time I can spend on the new parts I've never written.

I know what you're thinking, "Why don't you build a proposal database?" We all try. Everyone thinks it's a great idea, and I'm sure some providers have been successful. But here's the problem. We respond to dozens of proposals each year, and each one uses a different team or different collection of people through the organization. And, like it or not, every RFP is different. Why? Because none of your needs are the same! Let's emphasize again why the client conversation is so fundamental. No matter how rich our proposal database, each response must be customized to the client's needs. Otherwise, you end up with a *great looking* marketing piece, without substance.

DUMP THE Q&A. MAKE A CALL INSTEAD.

Most of the formal RFPs also include a Q&A period. That's typically the formal method of avoiding the client interviews. I understand that you solicited 15 providers and it's a hassle to entertain calls from all of them. That understandable, but I made my point earlier about interviews. Do them! At times, the Q&A is helpful, predominately at clarifying the details required to do the pricing, but that's about it. Most of the time, the provider *makes up* a few questions to show a good faith effort to participate, and occasionally when we're feeling clever, we'll throw in some competitive trap questions we know other competitors can't answer. Most of the time, the Q&A isn't very useful; with all due respect, most the time the buyer misses their deadline for Q&A responses. Now, in good times, this causes the timeline to be extended. We like that. In bad times, the timeline stays as is, even though the answers are late. This leads to one of two outcomes: Either we're out of time and have to ignore any new information, or we work all weekend to completely rewrite a section based on the new clarifying information. It's the buyer's choice, but it seems to me that the better my providers know my needs, the better their response and the better my chances of success. So take your time.

We once lost a project because our proposal was time stamped at 5:02 p.m. when the due date was 5:00 p.m. Now, two points. First, it was a very difficult proposal to write. The buyer was a subdivision within a pharmaceutical company dealing with some hairy compliance issues, so I needed to make sure our solution was spot-on. It also required detailed solution descriptions that, in turn, required that I assign my most experienced designer, who of course was already assigned to another client (ironically within the same soliciting company). All that aside, here's my second point. Over the following five years, my company would become this client's preferred provider for training development—the overall company, not just the subdivision who originally solicited us. Lesson learned, we were the right partner for this deal, but the artificial requirements of the timeline led the buyer to pick another provider.

On the other hand, I recently responded to a RFP for a series of marketing courses. The RFP was fairly short, a couple pages discussing the business intent. This was followed by three conversations with the client, each about one hour. The project was complex; they were trying to head off waste due to promoting products from R&D to marketing that tended to fail in the market. They were changing their processes and adding some new techniques in market research. We needed a strong, clearly articulated approach and a good subject matter expert to complement our team. We spent about four weeks on the proposal before everyone was happy with it. We did win, the project was successful, and it is one of my favorites to talk about.

PRICING

Okay, then there is the pricing. Now this is the hard part. The first thing on the sales team's mind is to ensure that we are not pricing it too high, thus losing to a lower priced competitor. On the other hand, the first thing on the minds of the development team is that we are not pricing it too low, thus not leaving enough budget for the labor necessary to complete the work. There lies the rub.

This topic is complex. First off, the experience level of the buyer challenges the provider. Does the buyer have experience with training development outsourcing? It's not the same as outsourcing customer service, manufacturing, accounting, etc. Performance is not based on the number of transactions. In fact, the training industry has no standard for performance, nor a standard process for doing the work. How did the buyer gain the expectation of the pricing? Did the buyer get the baseline for the pricing from an industry publication?

Pricing may be the biggest challenge in the outsourcing relationship. It's a very big challenge and any service oriented business. If all of the development projects were on a time and materials basis, then it would be less challenging. We would simply quote a rate for each type of person that would be assigned to the account and then multiply that rate times the number of hours they worked. But it's never that simple. In fact in the learning development business nearly all of the projects are on a fixed based price.

If we were selling products, such as the manufacturing of credit cards or tires or any other type of physical product, and pricing for an outsourcing account that involved a volume of this product would simply be the cost of the development of one of these products, plus the margin that we would expect to earn on that product, and then multiplied by the number of products that were to be developed, minus perhaps some percentage for the economy of scale gained with a large volume. It would be a simple pricing exercise and you have a fairly consistent ability to hit those costs and those margins. However training development is not that simple. No two projects are like. One project may cost X number of dollars to develop while the other projects, which is of similar length, may take one half X, or X +1, or X * 2 based on all the factors involved in the course development process. Later, I will address all these factors and how they come to play in the pricing.

The expectation for procurement is to use the lowest priced provider. The expectation for the buyer is to choose the client who best meets their needs, at the best price. Price is a big deal, however, I will echo often that price *must not be* the buyer's deciding factor. The cliché is that "you get what you pay for", and in training development that is often true. I've lost many proposals to competitors with lower costs, but I've also won many when I was the *highest* cost provider because I was a better fit for the buyer's needs. These were situations where the project was mission critical, quality was vital, and they only had one chance to get it right. In this case, the buyer wants expertise, not a good deal. Did the buyer simply write a bigger check? No, it usually took some serious conversation, compromise, and a bit of haggling to get to the final price. I'll emphasize this often. You must choose the provider who best meets your needs, <u>and</u>

then negotiate. If you choose simply based on price, then you will get a low price, but you are likely to also get low quality, the provider's least expensive (experience or talented) staff, and a lot of grief about cost overruns.

INITIAL INTERVIEW QUESTIONS

Below is the series of questions that I have been using for over a decade during the initial client interview. It provided a strong understanding of the client's current state and their needs. Most of all, it sparked the right conversations to make sure we could produce the best proposal.

1. What is your vision for the course? (Have them explain the background.)
2. What problems are you trying to solve? What situation you are trying to prepare for?
3. Is this part of a larger business strategy (product roll-out, change program, etc.)?
4. Who is the audience? How many? What are their characteristics?
5. What's your anticipated length of the course?
6. If this is a system course, is the system done? If it is not, when will it be stable enough to include screenshots in the course?
7. Is this a conversion of an ILT course? If so, is the instructor available as needed?
8. If this is a blended solution, then when is the ILT?
9. Is content available; if so, in what format?

10. Who are the SMEs? Where are they located? Are they available for the amount of time we'll need?

11. Who are the stakeholders?

12. Who has approval authority? Will it require a Legal review?

13. Do you anticipate any foreign localization requirements?

14. What is the delivery strategy? What LMS are they using?

15. What are your expectations for the interface? If this is an existing client, can we use a previous one?

16. What is the expected media level?

17. Are there existing course standards?

18. Are there specific technical requirements such as book marketing, filtering, or assessment tracking?

19. How soon do they want to kick off the project?

20. When is it due? What is driving the timeline/due date?

21. Is the scope driven by quality, timeline, budget, or another business priority?

22. Given the wide range of solutions that we could build, are there are many budget parameters we need to make sure we stay within?

Chapter 11

Pricing Strategies

This is the hard part. The first thing on the sales team's mind is to ensure that we are not pricing our training solution too high, thus losing to a lower-priced competitor. On the other hand, the first thing on the minds of the development team is that we are not pricing it too low, thus not leaving enough budget for the labor necessary to complete the work. Therein lies the rub.

This topic is complex. First, the experience level of the buyer challenges the provider. Does the buyer have experience with training development outsourcing? It's not the same as outsourcing customer service, manufacturing, accounting, etc. Performance is not based on the number of transactions. In fact, the training industry has no standard for performance, nor a standard process for doing the work. How did the buyer figure the expectation of the pricing? Did the buyer get the baseline for the pricing from an industry publication?

Pricing may be the biggest challenge in the outsourcing relationship. It's a very big challenge in any service-oriented business. If all development projects were on a time-and-materials basis, then it would be less challenging. We would simply quote a rate for each type of person who would be assigned to the account and multiply that rate times the number of hours they worked. However, it's never that simple. In fact, in the learning development business, nearly all the projects are on a fixed-based price.

If we were selling products, such as the manufacturing of credit cards or tires or any other type of physical product, and pricing for an outsourcing account that involved a volume of this product, it would simply be the cost of the development of one of these products, plus the margin that we would expect to earn on that product, and then multiplied by the number of products that were to be developed, minus perhaps some percentage for the economy of scale gained with a large volume. It would be a simple pricing exercise, and you have a fairly consistent ability to hit those costs and margins. However, training development is not that simple. No two projects are like. One project may cost X number of dollars to develop, while other projects of similar length may take $\frac{1}{2}X$ or $X + 1$ or $X*2$ based on all the factors involved in the course development process. I will address all these factors and how they come to play in the pricing.

The expectation for procurement is to use the lowest-priced provider. The expectation for the buyer is to choose the client who best meets their needs, at the best price. Price is a big deal; however, I will echo often that price *must not be* the buyer's deciding factor. The cliché "You get what you pay for" is often true in training development. I've lost many proposals to competitors with lower costs, but I've also won many when I was the *highest-cost* provider because I was a better fit for the buyer's needs. These were situations where the project was mission critical, quality was vital, and they only had one chance to get it right. In this case, the buyer wants expertise, not a good deal. Did the buyer simply write a bigger check? No, it usually took some serious conversation, compromise, and a bit of haggling to get to the final price. I'll emphasize this. You must choose the provider who best meets your needs and then negotiate. If you choose based solely on price, then you will get a low price, but you are likely to also get low quality, the provider's least expensive (experience or talented) staff, and lots of grief about cost overruns.

PRICING STRATEGIES

One of the top issues with pricing is its direct impact on the health of the vendor's business. This is crucial for a small, growing company and even a very large company with growth targets that they must meet. If you set the price too high, then the sales leads and executives will fear that we won't get the business. If you price the projects too high, then they will all fear the loss of the account to a lower-cost competitor. On the other hand, the operations and development teams fear that if you set the cost too low, they will not have the budget, time, hours, and ability to afford the qualified resources that it takes to fulfill the customer's needs. So the trick is to find that sweet spot. Find the highest price that the customer is willing to pay, and model that price so that the development teams can safely execute and achieve the client's vision. This is indeed were lots of accounts either succeed or fail.

I stated earlier in the book (in fact, I stated it multiple times) that it is a true mistake to select a vendor simply because they are the lowest-cost provider. As we've outlined throughout the book, there is a huge gap between those vendors who can align with your organization and fulfill your needs and those who are unable to align with your organization and to fill even your basic needs, no matter how great they look during the sales presentation. Thus, while cost is always important, it cannot be the deciding factor in a relationship. You must select your vendor along the Seven Attributes and then negotiate. The vendor will give you their best price. It only takes the process of negotiation to determine what that price is.

If I was ever successful in anything in the training outsourcing business, it may had been in determining the right price and then aligning and operational team that could meet the client's needs within those parameters. As a small boutique firm, we were like a surgical unit as opposed to general practitioner. We had fewer clients, but we were given the specialty cases—the really challenging business problems to solve; we would assign high-caliber talent to the projects, so we cost more than other providers. As a small company, this was a luxury that we could afford. We didn't need hundreds of projects, and our clients didn't have hundreds of projects to give us. All we needed was a strong price base and the ability to produce a consistent margin to support the handful of people we had on our roster. Once we began to grow and upon the acquisition of my company by one of the larger providers, we began to compete for the much larger accounts. These are the accounts where the client <u>did</u> have hundreds of projects that needed to be developed, and where I would need many more employees to execute on that goal. In that scenario, the client is not going to pay top dollar—the amount our previous clients might have. They had large volumes, and they wanted the discount associated with those volumes.

At that time, I was forced to determine a model where I could still provide the level of quality that I believed necessary, a level of quality that reflected our reputation and enabled us to continue to grow, while still meeting the client's goal of a lower-cost solution. That was a challenge I needed to overcome.

My first big test was a multimillion dollar account with one of the world's largest financial services companies. While they had hundreds of courses they would assign to us, there were only three categories of course—high, medium, and low. This is a situation that every vendor faces. What is a high-level course?

What is a low-level course? The courses that we would be assigned would range from compliance courses to product roll-out training to systems integration training, and all points in between. No two courses would be the same. If we were developing hundreds of compliance courses, then we would expect some degree of consistency and boilerplate approach that we could use for each course, but that was never the case. Every course has a different subject matter, which meant different subject matters experts with which to build relationships. Many courses would be of different modalities: classroom, online, quick reference guides, self-study, etc. The complexity of the business problem that needed to be solved most definitely varied from course to course.

DEFINING COMPLEXITY

So the challenge to the vendor is how to encapsulate their definition of high, medium, and low and to determine a single fixed-price for every solution that will fit into that category. This is one circumstance where the more complicated you make it, the safer you will be. You will frequently find yourself in the situation of determining which category the solution fits into and how that category is defined, and forming an agreement with the client that the scope of this request fits cleanly within the definition of the category by which it is being priced. The client may arrive with a request they feel is a low-level training program, but after assessing the criteria, they may identify that one or more of the factors are of a higher level that changes the overall training program from low to medium. That simple exercise may have saved the project, especially if you go in with a false assumption that is a low-level project and then find out that perhaps the SMEs are unavailable on a regular basis, or it's a systems training project but the system isn't completed and won't be completed until shortly before the delivery of the training, or that the subject matter is a new business initiative where the overall description and details of that initiative have never been documented. These are simply a few examples of the criteria within the project that will indeed determine the time it takes to complete the project and the number of hours it will take to complete the work. If you go with a simple assumption that it's a low-level project because it has less media, yet the project takes four weeks longer than expected because, for example, you have to fall in line with the development of the information system, then you will incur some factor of four extra weeks of labor in addition to what you had planned for a typical low-level project. The result is that you will be over budget on that project, and the vendor eats the costs or the vendor has to renegotiate the project midstream. Neither makes both sides happy. These situations can largely be avoided if you follow an effective pricing strategy.

I have been fortunate to work with some of the leading companies in this world. And over the course of building these relationships and encountering so many different permutations of a training program, I had to become increasingly more strategic in my pricing. I had to apply a formula of cause and effect to the way I approach pricing. The price is a result of the labor and costs that are required to complete the project—in other words, to complete the construction of the *product* that the vendor has been contracted to create. The number of hours needed to contribute to completion of that product is a direct result of the components, elements, and makeup of that product. In order to come up with a price that will consistently result in a successful project and enable the vendor to generate a profit, you must be very specific about what you will be building, the components and elements that will be included, and the levels of complexity involved in the environment.

DEFINING A MODEL

Two of the companies that I've had the fortune to work with were Microsoft and Bank of America. There are only a few companies on this planet larger than these two companies, and I will assume from my experience that there only a few companies in the world as complex as these two companies. I had the fortune of working with both companies on some very large engagements. While I continued to hone my pricing strategies over the last 14 years, regarding what worked and what would help my teams be successful, the experience with Microsoft and

Bank of America really laid the groundwork for the models that I've been using.

In 2007, my team was contracted by Microsoft to help them formulate a new standard within their sales and marketing division that would enable them to be more successful in the usage of vendors to develop their courseware. This involved a number of outcomes, including the development of a platform that every vendor would use to create the courseware. It also produced a definition and structure by which Microsoft vendors would classify high-, medium-, and low-complexity products. I then used that model when we established the relationship with Bank of America. We took the Bank of America model and integrated the other components that we had identified through the Microsoft model to come up with a structure that, in many ways, helped ensure that we very accurately classified training requests, the types of training requests, and any associated effort necessary to create those products, ensuring that the price we would be charging for that product was in line with the effort it would take to build it.

Every year, there is a new survey and a new presentation by any one of the research agencies that attempts to summarize what the prevailing cost per hour currently is for training programs. They attempt to dissect different training programs such as online, classroom, self-study, and so on, and they attempt to summarize requests as high, medium, and low. Unfortunately, the prevailing metric that is used to determine high, medium, and low is the interactivity or media included. The assumption is that if a program has lots of graphics and animations, that particular course must be high complexity. Likewise, if the course only uses text to present the content, has no audio, and has limited interactivity, that course was of low complexity and therefore a cheaper price. It's not that simple.

So what are the conditions that impact the complexity of the training program? They include:

- The level of Bloom's taxonomy
- The overall project's complexity (not product)
- The condition of the business processes being addressed
- The aggressiveness of the timeline
- The complexity of the solution (linear, role-based, learner-directed, etc.)
- The complexity of the navigation
- The state of the content sources (all existing, all new, or in between)
- The ability of the SME
- The condition of the system, if it's a system course
- The existence of any templates required
- The level of media
- The requirement for audio
- The complexity of the knowledge checks

- The complexity of the comprehensive assessment, if any
- The requirement for tracking
- The technology being used

I'm sure that there may be others, especially as the technical alternatives for learning solutions continue to expand (mobile, social, PSS, etc.), but this clearly illustrates that the definition of high-, medium-, and low-complexity and the resulting prices are much more complex than simply the level of media included.

To summarize my insider's advice for appropriate pricing: Make sure the vendors clearly understand your needs, give them ample time to produce a clear response, and make sure your pricing expectations and model consider all the factors involved in the very complex process of training development.

Conclusion

I haven't seen it all, but I've seen a lot. Trying to summarize 14 years or so in the learning industry has been challenging, but I consider it rewarding. By the time this book is published, it will be nearly one year since that presentation at the CLO Symposium that resulted in this book (and my new business). The process has given me the chance to reflect on some of the more impressive successes I had a chance to witness and think about the teams and the people involved, the things they did right, the way the teams work together, and the impressive results they were able to achieve. Often this occurred under normal conditions, but it's most impressive when you see occur in the high-stress or rushed conditions that we so often experience in today's business.

I hope the case studies and anecdotes I've shared will help both the potential clients and the prospective vendors form an alignment that allows each to be successful. The Seven Attributes, in my opinion, will greatly assist the buyer's ability to produce an effective RFP and identify the right partner. Applying the nuances of the Seven Attributes will also allow the vendor and the client to form an alignment in a constructive relationship. I'd further suggest that a solid study of each attribute can lead to improvement opportunities for any vendor and increase their competitive ability.

What we do is very hard. There's no question about it. No two projects look the same. No two clients have the same needs. So identifying a perfect partner who fits each unique need and has the capability of producing a long-term ***trusted*** relationship is a foremost challenge in any business and for any individual who has been asked to make this choice.

ABOUT THE AUTHOR

William V. West has 30 years experience in change management, learning technologies, and entrepreneurship; with a concentration in custom development and outsourcing since 2001. His expertise includes the development of elearning, mlearning, social media, VILT, vendor selection, and learning platforms. He has served over 50 corporate clients; including eighteen within the Fortune 150 and the largest company in eleven of the top industry sectors. He held leadership positions in some of the L&D industry's most influential companies: Accenture, E&Y, Option Six, GP Strategies, and Xerox. His teams have earned 20 international awards while creating over 1,000 custom learning solutions. He also won twelve regional and state awards for entrepreneurship and was recognized for three consecutive years in the Inc. 5000. His work in elearning has also appeared on CBS 60 minutes as "the potential of elearning".

West is currently founder of QuantumConnect, whose mission is to help learning organizations and consulting providers to improve their performance and their competitive ability. His recent publication, Seven Attributes of Highly Effective

Development Vendors, has received high accolades from media and some of the world's leading companies.

William West is available for speaking engagements, consulting, and conducts workshops for companies looking to succeed in tactical initiatives, such as:

- Start-up: The entrepreneurial success

- Now what: Operationalizing mergers and acquisitions

- Comparing an Apple to a Zebra: Selecting the best outsourcing provider

- The Next Step: Implementing a successful outsourcing relationship

- E-Learning past, present and future: Creating highly efficient development environments

- Landing whales: Writing great proposals and winning the big ones!

- Running Learning like a Business: Three pillars of success: standards, infrastructure, resourcing

Contact Information:
William V. West
Email: wvwest@wvwest.com
Twitter @WILLIAMVWEST
linkedin WILLIAMVWEST